The

TRADEHARD.COM™

Guide to Conquering the Trading Markets

M. GORDON PUBLISHING GROUP

Los Angeles, California

ISBN 1-893756-02-5

Printed in the United States of America

CHAPTER 3

How I Trade Momentum Stocks   **39**

by Jeff Cooper

CHAPTER 4

How I Use Historical Volatility to Identify Market Explosions   **51**

by Larry Connors

CHAPTER 5

The Key to Capturing Profits in the Option Markets   **57**

by Robert Pisani, Ph.D.

Chapter 6

My Three Favorite Trend Strategies   **71**

by Dave Landry

CONTENTS

Disclaimer

It should not be assumed that the methods, techniques, or indicators presented in this book will be profitable or that they will not result in losses. Past results are not necessarily indicative of future results. Examples in this book are for educational purposes only. The author, publishing firm, and any affiliates assume no responsibility for your trading results. This is not a solicitation of any order to buy or sell.

The NFA requires us to state that "HYPOTHETICAL OR SIMULATED PERFORMANCE RESULTS HAVE CERTAIN INHERENT LIMITATIONS. UNLIKE AN ACTUAL PERFORMANCE RECORD, SIMULATED RESULTS DO NOT REPRESENT ACTUAL TRADING. ALSO, SINCE THE TRADES HAVE NOT ACTUALLY BEEN EXECUTED, THE RESULTS MAY HAVE UNDER- OR OVERCOMPENSATED FOR THE IMPACT, IF ANY, OF CERTAIN MARKET FACTORS, SUCH AS LACK OF LIQUIDITY. SIMULATED TRADING PROGRAMS IN GENERAL ARE ALSO SUBJECT TO THE FACT THAT THEY ARE DESIGNED WITH THE BENEFIT OF HINDSIGHT. NO REPRESENTATION IS BEING MADE THAT ANY ACCOUNT WILL OR IS LIKELY TO ACHIEVE PROFITS OF LOSSES SIMILAR TO THOSE SHOWN."

About TRADEHARD.COM

A trader who retired from the markets only two decades ago would hardly recognize the business today. The Dow was still below 1000, Treasury bond futures had just been born, and personal computers were cumbersome, expensive machines of interest mostly to subscribers of *Popular Science*. The World Wide Web did not even exist; the Internet was an obscure communications network known only to a small community of government and military personnel, defense contractors, and academics.

In short, the computer age was in its infancy and had yet to make the sweeping changes in financial exchange operation, communications, data distribution, market analysis, and trade entry we take for granted today. It is only a mild exaggeration to say the trading industry has changed more in the last two decades than it had in the previous ten. What has remained constant, though, is the need for timely, reliable information to make trading decisions.

TRADEHARD.COM was designed with that need in mind. It is a cutting-edge Internet site that provides trading strategies, technical indicators, market commentary, price information, and other essential resources from a blue-chip roster of established traders who make their livings buying and selling in the markets. TRADEHARD.COM is a complete online trading center developed *by* traders *for* traders, complemented by a series of informative and clearly written books. Whether you are a novice or a market professional, TRADEHARD.COM, offers you a place on the Internet where you can find the information and services you need to keep on top of today's markets.

Our approach is simple. We show you how highly successful stock, futures, and options traders go about making money—the strategies they use and the insights they have gained from years of firsthand experience in the markets. In addition to daily market, indicator, and strategy updates, TRADEHARD.COM offers a fully interactive and constantly updated menu of quotes, charts, news, educational articles, trader forums and interviews, message boards, and online technical and research tools.

Because computers and the Internet have become integral to successful trading, the Web provides the perfect vehicle for providing comprehensive and timely trading information. Our goal is to make the most of this medium's potential. Rather than going to one source for one piece of

CHAPTER 10

What Top Traders Know 143

CHAPTER 11

Reaching the Trading Pinnacle 155

APPENDIX

The New Trading Technology and the TRADEHARD.COM Web Site 159

trading information and a different source for another, we offer you everything you need under one "virtual roof."

The TRADEHARD.COM Guide to Conquering the Trading Markets is designed to complement our Web site. It explains the trading approach of the TRADEHARD.COM cofounders, discusses the importance of money management, overviews the current state of the trading industry (what you need to know about today's markets, technology, and online trading, etc.), and most important of all, offers a wealth of specific trading strategies and tactics from the professional traders who share their expertise every day on the Web site. We strive to bring you fresh insights and practical advice, and tell you the facts about trading many other books conveniently gloss over. Regardless of your skill level or approach, you will find what you need to hone your trading skills and apply them more successfully in the markets. *The TRADEHARD.COM Guide to Conquering the Trading Markets* is only the first in a series of books that will help you maximize your trading potential and take advantage of the wealth of features on the TRADEHARD.COM site.

Future books will explore more, and more specific, aspects of trading and the markets—always with an eye on industry developments and the importance of integrating materials with our Web site. Through our Web site and books, we look forward to providing you with the highest-quality professional trading resources.

Getting a Trading Edge

Anyone who has spent time in the financial markets has inevitably heard traders use the word "edge"—something that gives them an advantage in the competitive world of trading. One trader's edge might be a trading system he has designed, another trader's might be the ability to keep cool and think clearly in volatile market conditions, and still another trader's might be low commissions and access to the best broker in a particular trading pit.

In the information age, however, the most important commodity is knowledge—more specifically, knowledge gained through experience. And when it comes to the markets, the only way to gain experience is to trade. The edge provided by having learned firsthand how markets really behave, what works and what does not in trading, and how to accept losses unemotionally and capture profits efficiently, cannot be underestimated. Unfortunately, many, if not most, trading books are academic exercises (or even worse, casual observations) written by non-traders—analysts, newsletter writers, and an assortment of market commentators, gurus, and economic "theoreticians"—with no experience risking real money or making real profits in the markets.

While not all the ideas in such books can be automatically dismissed as useless (many analysts and commentators have legitimate trading insights), ultimately there is no substitute for hands-on experience. Trading is not just about understanding market concepts, it is about making decisions and acting on them—and the only way to get better is through experience. After all, if you wanted to become a major league pitcher, who would you want to learn from, a Cy Young winner with a 95-m.p.h. fastball, or a physicist who can accurately describe the aerodynamic forces at work in a well-thrown pitch? The physicist may be infinitely more intelligent, better educated, and more knowledgeable about the *science* of pitching, but he's never been on the mound in the bottom of the ninth with the bases loaded and a full count.

By the same token, who would you want to teach you about trading, salaried market gurus who never put their own money where their mouths are or real traders who have developed concrete strategies based on years of experience in the markets? Whose advice is more important to you, that of analysts with no stake in their forecasts or true market professionals who make their living day in and day out by risking their own money? It's not a tough choice if you think about it for a minute.

The concept behind this book is to give you access to the strategies and insights of established traders who pay their bills by taking profits out of the markets. The material in this book represents the accumulated market wisdom of seven professional traders with combined experience of nearly a century in the stock, futures, and options markets. They bring blue-chip track records and invaluable lessons about what it takes to survive, and ultimately prosper, in the financial markets.

Quite simply, these are major-league traders. Kevin Haggerty, former manager of U.S. equity trading for Fidelity Investments; Mark Boucher, top-rated hedge fund manager, author, and lecturer; Manuel Ochoa, one of the hottest new hedge fund managers, specializing in the S&P 500 and T-bonds; Robert Pisani, Ph.D., developer of the option "Greeks," and founder of one of the original options trading firms; trader and *Hit and Run Trading* author Jeff Cooper, who specializes in short-term stock trading, and traders Larry Connors and Dave Landry, who have done cutting-edge work in the area of volatility trading. All the contributors use common-sense language and clear trade examples.

We're not trying to offer you a "holy grail" for trading success. There are no dubious claims of turning your $5,000 trading account into $1 million in two months *with absolutely no risk!* We simply give you the practical trading approaches of market professionals. Instead of discussing abstract theories or hypothetical terms (how things "can be" or "might be"), they tell you how things really are. Instead of vague suggestions about how to buy and sell, the traders in the pages will simply tell you, "This is how we do it," using practical trading examples to clearly illustrate the techniques they use.

Endless repetition of the supposed merits of a particular indicator or technique can result in a large number of traders blindly accepting ideas with little or no practical value. Successful trading, however, is knowing when to buck the herd. Many of the accepted truths of trading in general, and using technical indicators in particular, are completely unfounded. We try to give you unique indicators and original trading techniques developed by practicing traders, as well as new techniques using familiar indicators that fly in the face of conventional wisdom.

The TRADEHARD.COM Guide to Conquering the Trading Markets is easy enough for beginners to understand, but it will appeal to even the most advanced traders—anyone interested in expanding their technical trading skills and learning fresh trading approaches will benefit from this book. We cover a number of topics: general discussions on the markets and current trading technology, risk control and money management, trading systems, and explanations of some of the indicators and techniques from our Web site. Finally, there are pages and pages of clear, detailed trading strategies, principles, and observations from top traders. We also will touch on some of the "intangibles" that so many other books overlook, but which often mean the difference between seat-of-your pants gambling and well-informed trading.

What you see is what you get: Real trading insight from real traders; practice instead of theory. Throughout the book, the emphasis is on the realities of trading rather than wishful thinking. That's what it's all about.

CHAPTER 1

Trading versus Investing: The Big Picture

In our age of split-second communications and information overload, it is ironic that there is such a shortage of reliable trading information. The market is flooded with misleading or inaccurate magazine articles and books, as well as materials that assume a level of expertise (or stupidity) on the part of the reader that may not exist.

Traders come in many shapes and sizes. Many new traders are motivated by a desire to take charge of their investments and maximize their returns. Others are enticed by tales of fortunes made in the markets or the dream of a full-time trading career. The vast majority of these individuals view trading as a natural extension of the "buy-

and-hold" investing they did in the past, and they approach it from a traditional, fundamental vantage point—analyzing a company's financial balance sheet to determine if its stock is undervalued, weighing supply and demand factors to evaluate commodities, and so on.

For the most part, though, such neophytes enter the markets blindly, not understanding the differences between investing and trading—or how the two differ from gambling, for that matter. If they hang on long enough to become successful (95–97 percent of futures traders, for example, are estimated to lose money), they will have learned to appreciate the differences between these endeavors—a lesson every potential trader should know *before* risking money in the markets.

Trading, investing, gambling: Are they simply different names for the same thing?

Hardly, although all investing and trading is gambling, in the sense that you are by definition placing your money at risk with absolutely no guarantee of profit. Past returns, while they may be useful as a general barometer of your odds, are definitely not indicative of future returns, as the standard brokerage industry disclaimer states. The differences between these endeavors have more to do with your goals and the way you try to achieve them than with the nature of the game being played.

The easiest to understand is gambling. When the average person goes to Las Vegas or Atlantic City, he or she goes there for entertainment. Playing blackjack, shooting craps, or spinning the roulette wheel offers excitement and diversion. The attitude of the typical vacationer in Las Vegas is usually, "I'll go golfing or sit by the pool this afternoon, see the Elvis impersonator after dinner, and then blow $200 in the casino." You may read up on a few blackjack strategies, but making money is not the goal—having fun is. If you happen to make a few bucks in the process, great, but we all know that for every person who hits the jackpot, there are a thousand others who lost enough money to make up the difference, and then some—that is how the casinos make their money. The goal of gambling is diversion, and the gambler's approach is generally casual—there is no plan involved.

This puts trading and investing in a much clearer perspective. While many people find trading and investing enjoyable, their primary focus (if they are smart) is not on entertainment, but on making money. This goal—to profit—is the most important difference between trading and investing versus gambling. But to succeed, traders and investors must also differ from the gambler by having a plan to achieve their goals. By far the most common mistake of the beginner is to approach the markets casually, like a gambler. Developing a well-researched plan based on solid knowledge of the markets is critical to successful trading.

So how does the trader differ from the investor? Here the distinctions are more subtle, but more important. The goal for both is to make money—either as supplemental income or as the primary source of income—and the method for serious traders and investors is deliberate; that is, a plan is involved. The investor, however, commonly takes a long-term perspective (5, 10, or 20 or more years into the future) on the markets and seeks to buy what he thinks are valuable assets (usually stocks) and hold them in the expectation they will increase in value. This traditional "buy-and-hold" investor is encouraged by the media and a slew of economists and financial professionals who tout the historical long-term performance of the stock market as evidence of it being both the most prudent and profitable investment vehicle (assuming of course, that the average investor is primarily concerned with saving for retirement). They are advised to "ride out" downturns in the market—ignore losses in the faith they will recoup them over the long haul.

The trader (or speculator), on the other hand, takes a more active approach. He seeks to improve returns and minimize risk by taking advantage of shorter-term price moves (shorter-term, that is, compared to the buy-and-hold approach) that also offer the opportunity to trade both sides of the market—thereby avoiding losing money (and even having the opportunity to make money) during market downturns. Traders vary significantly in terms of their strategies, the length of their trades, their methods of controlling risk, etc. A floor trader in a busy stock, futures, or options pit may buy and sell more than a hundred times a day, with an average trade lasting perhaps 20 seconds. A commodity trading advisor (CTA) managing hundreds of millions of dollars using a longer-term trading system may have positions that last more than a year. Most traders fall somewhere between these extremes. The techniques traders use to identify buy and sell points, as well as methods to curtail losses and maximize profitability, are the ultimate subject of this book.

A final word on trading versus gambling: Some people do trade because of the excitement; they will almost all be ex-traders before long. If you are in trading for the excitement, for the adrenaline, you will certainly be rewarded—every way except financially. Economic ruin can indeed be an extremely "exciting" experience.

THE BUY-AND-HOLD MYTH

The buy-and-hold investment approach is accepted without question by millions of investors who neither demand any proof of its validity nor consider the possibility of something better. Hand in hand with the acceptance of the buy-and-hold philosophy is the dismissal of any kind of "market timing," which usually implies technical analysis. (Never mind that the profitability of the fundamental analysis used to evaluate stocks is more difficult to verify historically than that of many technical trading approaches.) You cannot beat the market, they say. Better to just ride out the storm and accept any market downturns as part of the price of playing the game.

There are a couple ways to look at this. If you are 30 years old and retirement is potentially 30 or more years in the future, and you believe in the buy-and-hold approach, you never need to read a book, magazine article, company financial report, or newspaper (or watch the news) ever again, as far as your investments are concerned. You only need to funnel your money steadily into an equity index fund for the next few decades, and the statistics say you will eventually come out on top. If the market takes a downturn, so what? You will make your money back eventually.

But what if one of the downturns you have to "ride out" occurs two years before you were ready to retire, wiping out 20, 30, or 40 percent or more of your savings? Or, what if such a downturn occurs when you need money for yourself or your family in an emergency or even for something more mundane like a house or to start your own business? Will you be willing or able to wait 3, 5, or 10 years to recoup your losses? What if you were simply interested in improving your returns?

For those who consider the buy-and-hold method to be unassailable, consider this: From roughly 1966 to 1982—a period of 16 years—the U.S. stock market essentially remained flat in nominal terms (see Figure 1.1, which shows the Dow Jones Industrial Average from June 1, 1965, through June 1, 1984) and actually lost ground when adjusted for inflation. This would mean a 49-year-old in 1966 looking forward to retirement at age 65, with a substantial amount of his equity in stocks, would actually have been poorer by the time his company gave him his gold watch and good-bye party. Upon reflection, one might be tempted to say "buyer beware" regarding long-term stock holdings, but a more accurate admonition might be "holder beware."

This is not to say long-term stock investment is without merit. On the contrary, the statistical evidence of healthy historical stock market returns over the majority of 10-, 20-, and 30-year periods is compelling. But it is equally important to remember this approach is not foolproof and

FIGURE 1.1

Dow Jones Industrial Average—June 1, 1965–June 1, 1984

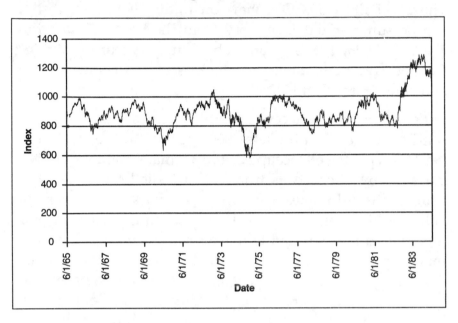

carries a significant amount of downside risk. It also ignores out of hand the possibility of enhancing returns through active trading, at least with a portion of your money (assuming some of it will remain committed to long-term stock holdings). Such improvements can be attained not only by identifying technical patterns that suggest profitable trades but also by trading markets (like most futures markets) that are simply impossible to trade with a buy-and-hold approach, by using leverage, and by trading both sides of the market—options not always available in traditional stock investing.

WHY WE TRADE INSTEAD OF INVEST

The TRADEHARD.COM view on trading versus investing can be summarized in a story from the book *Hit and Run Trading* (1996, M. Gordon Publishing) by cofounder Jeff Cooper, commentator in the stocks section of the Web site and contributor to this book.

Jeff's father was a successful textile businessman who, after retiring at age 42 in the late 1950s, turned to the stock market to keep himself occupied and to make money. He was barraged by phone calls from enthusiastic brokers who encouraged him to take long-term stock market positions and enhance his profit potential by purchasing stocks on margin. The brokers seemed to make sense—after all, they were market professionals—and he went along with the strategy. All was well—for awhile. Then, in 1962, on a day when his wife was being operated on for cancer, Mr. Cooper went bankrupt, his brokers liquidating his portfolio to meet margin calls. The family was wiped out and in debt to the brokerage houses. This was Jeff's first exposure to buy-and-hold investing.

Jeff's father, though, was determined to get his family back on its feet, and within five years he had built up and sold another multi-million dollar textile business. Next, he promised himself he would make back every cent he'd lost in the stock market. This time around, though, he kept his distance from the buy-and-hold strategy. After doing a great deal of research, he decided the most profitable game was to buy hot initial public offerings (IPOs) and sell them for small gains. Immediately, it worked: Within a few years,

Jeff's father was the largest IPO player on Wall Street and had made far more money than he had lost in 1962.

The story doesn't end here, though. When Jeff himself gravitated towards Wall Street in the 1980s, he initially tried to use his father's IPO strategy—but it didn't work. The market had changed; mutual funds were muscling out individuals in the IPO market. In the middle of the decade, Jeff transformed himself into a big-picture, buy-and-hold investor. Like his father, he was besieged by brokers who tried to direct him into stocks they were sure were absolute steals. The 1980s bull run that made geniuses out of so many people carried Jeff along for the ride, too, but in October 1987, he and many other buy-and-holders discovered the error of their ways. While not wiped out, the hit was substantial, and Jeff set about developing a stock market strategy that would free him from the errors he and his father had made.

After almost a decade, he has certainly succeeded. His strategy of trading rather than investing allows him to profit in both bull and bear markets. He uses simple techniques based on short-term price movement that, combined with knowledge of which stocks to use them in and tight risk control, removes the risk of future buy-and-hold disasters.

In short, while the Warren Buffets of the world garner most of the media attention, the evidence suggests the kinds of returns possible through trading cannot be matched by investing. Richard Dennis, Monroe Trout, Paul Tudor Jones—men who amassed millions in relatively short time periods—are just a few of the names that come to mind. As one trader profiled in *Futures* magazine said, "If you're not trading short-term, you're not trading to make the most money."

COMMON TRAITS OF SUCCESSFUL TRADERS

Despite the great differences in style and philosophy among traders, those who succeed share certain characteristics. The following list really represents the foundation upon which the rest of trading is built.

Adequate capitalization. Rarely mentioned (and not a character trait per se), it is the prerequisite that renders trading skills academic. Trading is about surviving numerous losses to benefit from the (usually) less frequent, but more sizable, winners. Without adequate capitalization, the best trading strategy in the world is worthless—like putting a Ferrari in the hands of a five-year-old. The reason most new traders fail is the same reason most new businesses in any area fail: lack of money. Winning traders treat trading like a business—requiring time, effort, and enough money to stay afloat until your "company" is paying for itself.

A goal and a plan. Whether they use a strictly mechanical trading system or a set of general trading principles, successful traders have concrete trading goals and logical plans (based on observations of market behavior) to reach them. They are realists; they do not wish or hope for trades to go their way, expect trading to be painless, or look for instant success or overnight millions. Through long study of the markets, they develop an idea of what is possible, establish reasonable trading goals, and implement a plan to achieve them.

Attention to risk control and money management. Even the most successful traders usually have more losing trades than winning trades. The key is to manage losses, so small ones do not become big ones. Any trader will tell you his risk control (stops, etc.) and money management strategies (i.e., deciding how many shares or contracts to commit to a particular trade) are more important than the actual buy and sell signals he uses.

The ability to accept losses. Having winning trades is easy. Part of being a market realist is understanding that losses are part of the game. You will not reap the benefits of the winners until you have mastered the art of accepting the losers. This is really the ability to admit when you are wrong, to get out of a trade without bruising your ego or destroying your confidence.

Patience and perseverance. One top commodity trading advisor (CTA) who trades hundred of millions of dollars in the futures markets weathered five straight losing years before he finally turned himself into a profitable trader (and that was after spending several years as only a moderately successful stock investor). Another successful trader spent the better part of 15 years researching, testing, and occasionally trading before putting a mechanical trading system to work in the markets. When he did, though, he turned less than $100,000 dollars into more than $1,000,000 in a year.

These examples are meant to illustrate a principle. Overnight riches, for the most part, do not occur in trading any more than they do in any other business—hype notwithstanding. Trading has a learning curve like any other subject. It takes years of training and on-the-job experience to become a competent surgeon, lawyer, musician or engineer; trading is no different.

Self-reliance. You have to have confidence in what you are doing. Do your own homework, and do not accept other traders' opinions as gospel. Base your trading on what makes sense to you about the markets. If you do not believe in what you are doing, you will not have the nerve to follow through on your trading plan—even if it is a potentially profitable one.

A WORD ON SYSTEMATIC VERSUS DISCRETIONARY TRADING AND THE STRATEGIES DESCRIBED IN THIS BOOK

A great number of trading ideas are described in this book. Some are systematic, others are discretionary, reflecting the trading styles of the TRADEHARD.COM cofounders.

This blend of systematic and discretionary techniques is representative of the industry as a whole, and it provides a rounded perspective on the markets. A systematic trader may introduce more discretion into his approach over time if he gains confidence in his decision-making abilities. On the other hand, a discretionary trader may hone his technique to the point that he can apply it systematically, and he may see emotional or financial benefits of doing so. One approach is not better than the other, and in truth, there is usually a great deal of overlap. Highly successful traders can be systematic or discretionary, or some combination of the two. Most systematic traders at least reserve the right to override a particular trade signal under certain circumstances, get out of a trade early, etc., and most discretionary traders usually have at least a few basic rules they follow and situations they like to capitalize on—they are not just flying by the seat of their pants.

Technical trading strategies do not have to be complex to be effective. In fact, in most cases, the simpler the strategy, the better it works. Remember, however, that absolutely no strategy is perfect (the ones presented in the following chapters are not) and you are always well-advised to conduct extensive research and testing on any strategy before you use it in the markets. The trading ideas we will share with you are just that—ideas—intended to give you a sense of the kinds of trading approaches that are possible.

The strategies in the following chapters are described using fairly specific, "systematic" steps for the sake of clarity and simplicity. They are not mechanical systems. Most of the techniques have an important discretionary element, which will be obvious when you read them. Even when specific stop or exit rules are stated, these should not necessarily be considered gospel—it is likely performance can be improved through familiarity and experience with these approaches; the rules simply provide the guidelines.

Trading Techniques of the TRADEHARD.COM Cofounders

In putting together this book, we thought a lot about what would really help working traders in their quest to conquer the markets. More descriptions of generic indicators, like those found in almost every other trading book? Nope. Hypothetical test results of super-long-term trend-following systems with 60 percent drawdowns that trade baskets of foreign bonds? Wrong again.

What we decided was to play our strongest hand. We asked the TRADEHARD.COM cofounders (Kevin Haggerty, Mark Boucher, Manuel Ochoa, Bob Pisani, Jeff Cooper, Larry Connors, and Dave Landry) to give us their best trading strategies, principles, and insights from their years in the trenches—the nuts and bolts of the methods and ideas that turned them into the winning traders they are today. This information is captured in Chapters 2 through 9.

Not surprisingly, it is an amazingly diverse collection of trading techniques, covering stocks, futures, and option markets, and everything from intraday strategies to trend-following approaches. But it quickly becomes apparent there are a handful of fundamental principles uniting this pool of talented traders:

1. They use specific technical price patterns that exploit inherent market principles.

2. They focus on momentum and trend continuation.

3. They use tight risk control.

4. They trade both sides of the market.

When you've finished reading the book, you'll understand why.

There's no mumbo-jumbo here—no talk of astrology, harmonic convergence cycles, or how tides affect prices. There are no useless platitudes like "never short stocks, only buy them" or get-rich-quick schemes that show you how you can consistently buy options at 1 and sell them at 10 three weeks later. These are not the kinds of things serious traders use to make money. Understanding market dynamics, how they are reflected in price, how to capitalize on them, and how to control risk, *are*. These are precisely the kinds of insights these top traders will share with you over the next seven chapters.

CHAPTER 2

Using Short-Term Strategies to Exploit Institutional Activity in the Stock Market

by Kevin Haggerty

Kevin Haggerty is a professional stock trader with more than u quarter-century of experience in the financial markets. From 1990 to 1997 he served as senior vice president and Manager of Equity Trading at Fidelity Capital Markets (a division of Fidelity Investments), where he was in charge of U.S. institutional equity trading and exchange floor operations.

Over the course of his career, Mr. Haggerty has held a number of high-profile positions: Managing Director of the Chicago Board

Options Exchange, member of the NYSE Stock Allocation Committee, member of the Chicago Stock Exchange board of governors, member of the NYSE "upstairs" trading advisory committee (U.T.A.C.), member of the S.I.A. Committee to advise the Securities and Exchange Commission on various aspects of the securities industry, and member of the National Organization of Investment Professionals (NOIP).

Prior to his tenure at Fidelity, Mr. Haggerty was a general partner in charge of equity and convertible trading at Walsh Greenwood from 1981 to 1990, where he also directed the sales and marketing of the "SHARK" system, the first personal computer-based equity and option trading quotation system. From 1976 to 1981, he was a vice president at Dean Witter-Reynolds and manager of equity and convertible trading.

Before entering the trading industry, Mr. Haggerty received his BS degree from Manhattan College, and served in the U.S. Marine Corps from 1965 to 1969. He achieved the rank of captain and was decorated for his service in the Vietnam War.

Mr. Haggerty currently uses his strategies to trade his personal account as well as his managed funds.

When you trade nearly a quarter of a century, you learn a thing or two about what really makes markets tick and the best way to profit from their basic characteristics. I've had an up-close look at how institutional traders play the markets, and I've found that what ultimately gives me an edge is matching the right price pattern to what the institutions are doing on any given day. Elephants cannot hide—price and volume give them away every time. Below I explain three strategies—Slim Jims, Devil's House, and Trap Doors—that reflect this philosophy. They are all quick-acting strategies that key off institutionally driven market action.

SLIM JIMS

If I could trade only one intraday pattern, it would be the Slim Jim (SJ), which is an intraday breakout of long, tight consolidations at or near the current day's high or low. These consolidations can take the form of horizontal trading ranges, slim triangles, or wedges, just below the high or low; the longer the consolidation, the better chance of an explosive move. One of the best things about SJs is that they give you a low risk, strong momentum, breakout play. By trading this pattern on big-name S&P issues, you capitalize on the momentum caused by institutional traders and program buyers piling into the market, forcing a breakout of the consolidation to new trading levels.

There are a number of factors I consider when deciding whether or not to take a trade, which I'll describe in terms of buy orders (just reverse all the rules that follow for short-selling situations):

1. The ideal stock should be trading above its (rising) 50- and 200-day moving averages.

2. I mostly use this strategy on the larger S&P 500 stocks because the following factors will be working in my favor:

- There will be institutional buyers.
- There will be program buyers.
- The specialist will probably be long; if he is, you can bet the stock will accelerate to the upside.
- Hedge funds will be trying to front-run the institutions.
- Institutions will be jumping ahead of other institutions.
- There will be normal technical buying by retail investors.

3. I like to see a minimum of 8 to 10 bars of consolidation on a five-minute bar chart (12 to 16 bars on a three-minute bar chat).

4. Price momentum and market dynamics are keys to timing your entry. Look for a stock trading on the offer side, with price and volume increasing on the time and sales screen, and, in the case of a Nasdaq stock, action on the market maker (level II) screen. I want to see market dynamics better at (or leading into) the breakout before I take the trade.

5. Enter on the first breakout of the consolidation and risk no more than 1/4 point. If you get stopped out, enter again if the stock does an "end-run," falling back into, or through, the consolidation before bursting through the original breakout level a second time.

Let's go over an example. Figure 2.1 shows a trade I took in Intel (INTC). It actually illustrates a variation of the pattern

FIGURE 2.1

Slim Jim: Intel, Five-Minute Bar

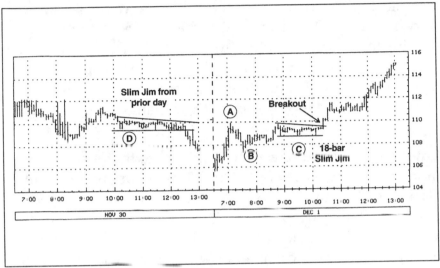

Source: Bloomberg LP.

known as Double Down, which is simply when a Slim Jim from the current day also breaks through the level of a Slim Jim from the prior day. Double Downs will sometimes give you a chance for what I call a "moon shot"—a 1 1/2 point (or bigger) profit on an intraday position.

All the pieces were in place. First, on December 1, 1998, INTC was trading above its 50- and 200-day moving averages (not shown), which meant I was working with an uptrending stock. Second, INTC is a big-name issue, which means the institutions, program buyers, hedge fund managers and market makers will all help drive the market action when a breakout occurs.

The action developed like this: INTC gapped down on the opening and then rallied to the 109 7/8–110 level (A). The tech stocks, which had led the initial morning rally, now sold off, and INTC (along with the S&P 500) retraced approximately half their initial up moves. INTC traded to the 109 level, forming an ascending triangle (B), then broke out to 109 3/8–109 1/2, and finally proceeded to form an 18-bar Slim Jim consolidation—a long, tight triangle near the day's high (C).

But there was another aspect of this trade that made it even more attractive. As the SJ formed, it was apparent a Double Down was coming into play: The stock was poised to breakout above the prior day's Slim Jim that had formed around the same price level (D). I went long on the breakout at 109 1/2 and "doubled down" on the position, buying twice as many shares as I would on a normal SJ. INTC then took off to new highs—a "moon shot!"

When multiple market players add fuel to the fire that a stock naturally experiences when it breaks out of a tight consolidation and through a significant resistance or support level, you can position yourself for low-risk, high-potential trade.

TRAP DOORS

This day-trading strategy is another great example of how understanding the interaction between specialists, institutions, and program buyers can put you on the inside track to great trades. Once I began to understand this characteristic of markets, I designed strategies to help me exploit it.

Trap Doors (TDRs) are long-side price momentum trades that I use to take advantage of emotional down openings that become overextended (the "trap door") and then snap back in the opposite direction as institutional buyers, program buyers, and specialists all drive the market to the upside. (I don't use this strategy to sell short because it is a fast technique and it's not easy to catch upticks.) Before we discuss the specific entry rules, let's look at a few interdependent factors that lay the groundwork for one of these trades.

Trade Criteria

These are the conditions I look for in a TDR setup:

1. I focus on market-leading stocks from the S&P 500 trading above $75 (I prefer those above $100). The ideal stock will not only be a market leader but will outperform the S&P 500 cash index.

2. The stock's average daily trading range must be a minimum of 1 1/2 points.

3. The stock's ADX must be greater than 25 and its 14-period RSI must be greater than 50.

4. The stock must be trading above its 50- and 200-day moving averages (the strongest stocks will be above their 20-day moving averages as well).

Entry Rules

If the conditions outlined above have been met, I enter the market using the following rules (described in terms of a five-minute bar chart):

1. The stock must open below the previous close and trade at least one point below the previous close.

2. After the opening bar, the second bar must make a lower high and a lower low.

3. Go long if the third bar trades above the high of the second. (This indicates the market isn't going to follow through on the "bad news" that caused the down opening, and a reversal may be in order.) This is the earliest you can enter the trade. Under normal conditions, you will enter on the fourth or fifth bar. (I'll explain why in a minute.)

I use very tight risk control and money management rules to get the most out of these trades. I like to limit risk to 1/4 point on a position. If the market does not prove me right quickly—when stronger market forces say "not this time"—I get out immediately and wait for another signal. Because TDRs will sometimes reverse and trade back in the direction of the opening, I try to sell half my position on the way up to cover costs and take a "feel-good profit." I then use a tight trailing stop to lock in profits on the remaining half of the position as I ride out the trend.

These are the basic entry rules, but several dynamic factors occurring as the trade develops will decide when (or if) I actually enter the market. A trade I took shown in Figure 2.2 (Merck) illustrates this perfectly. I've already mentioned that the third bar of the pattern is the earliest you can put on a TDR position. On December 3, 1998, the third bar of the pattern closed above the high of the second bar—the early TDR buy signal. However, I didn't enter the trade at that point because the following dynamic criteria hadn't shown sufficient strength:

- S&P futures starting to rally.

- NYSE ticks improving.

- Up volume/down volume ratio improving.

- Stock trading at the midpoint or ask side of the bid/ask spread.

- Bid size larger than the ask size.

- Volume increasing and transaction size getting bigger.

- Buy programs at level to kick in.

As a result, I waited until these pieces of the puzzle were in place before I took the trade.

This will give you an idea of what's happening in one of these situations and why this strategy works. When the specialist opens the "trap door" to take out the sellers on (and immediately after) the opening, he has incentive to push the stock back up to get his inventory position in shape. Also, institutions working scale-down buy orders as the market drops on the opening will turn around and chase the stock to the upside because they are afraid of missing a rally. Buy programs begin to kick in and the stage is set for the first good trade counter to the trap door opening.

Let's look at my trade from December 3, 1998 (Figure 2.2) in greater detail.

FIGURE 2.2
Trap Door: Merck, Five-Minute Bar

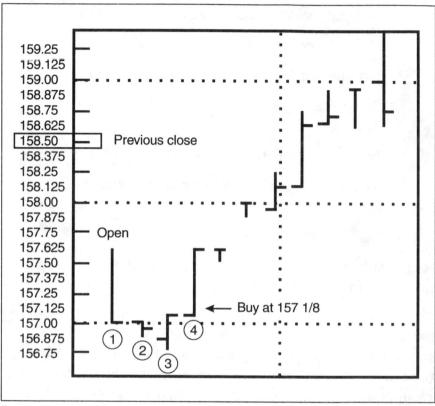

159.25
159.125
159.00
158.875
158.75
158.625
158.50 Previous close
158.375
158.25
158.125
158.00
157.875
157.75 Open
157.625
157.50
157.375
157.25
157.125 ← Buy at 157 1/8
157.00
156.875
156.75

① ② ③ ④

Source: Bloomberg LP.

1. The trap door is set when MRK opens at 157 5/8, down 7/8 from previous close of 158 1/2. (The volume on the open is 80,700 shares.) It quickly trades down to 156 13/16 on only 19,000 shares. This low volume helps create the vacuum that will make a reversal that much more forceful.

2. MRK trades at 156 13/16 and buyers start to enter the market.

3. The third bar closes at 157 1/16 (at its high) and above the high of bar two, giving the early buy signal (bar three trading above bar two). MRK is now trading at the midpoint of bid/ask spread and then quickly moves to the ask size, another indication of buying pressure (the bid has been raised three times at this point).

4. MRK is now offered at 157 1/8. When bar four trades above bar three (at 157 1/8), I go long, 1/16 over the bar three high. When I finally pulled the trigger on the trade, the following conditions existed:

   - NYSE ticks had increased by +200.
   - The S&P futures had started to rally.
   - Other key market leading stocks had also started to rally.
   - Buy programs were starting to kick in.
   - The stock had reached a level down 1 1/16 points from the previous close that began to attract some buyers.

The stage was then set to climb past the trap door and make some real money. Probabilities now favored the trade because the specialist wanted the stock to rally so he could move some inventory, buy programs were kicking in, and major S&P stocks were rallying. Institutions buying MRK had to move up with the rally and maintain their share of the market because the low-volume drop on the opening meant they had not bought enough stock at the lower levels.

Using the money management rules I talked about earlier, I sold half the position at 157 7/8 for a three-quarter-point profit. My trailing slop took me out of the remaining half of the position at 158 7/8 (on the way back down from the high of 159 1/4). The stock then proceeded to reverse and closed at 154 7/8.

Remember, when the three big "planets"—specialists, buy programs, and institutions—are lined up in your favor, quick action on and prudent risk control make TDRs high-probability trade opportunities.

DEVIL'S HOUSE

The final strategy I'll share with you is one I've been using for years. Every successful trader I know trades on the short side as well as the long side, and I'm no exception. The Devil's House (DH) is one of my favorite strategies to capture moves as prices decline.

The DH is a longer-term strategy that is based on a head-and-shoulders top pattern that forms *below* declining 200-, 50-, and 10-day moving averages. It's an explosive downside momentum pattern for stocks whose situations are bad and about to get worse (I've found that DHs often precede heavy volume blow-offs). Institutions will usually pull the plug on any remaining shares in their portfolios when the right shoulder of the pattern is broken and the market heads to new lows. (It might, for example, be the end of a reporting period, and they don't want to be caught holding this kind of declining stock.) The Devil's House is most commonly formed with a head-and-shoulders pattern, but the formation of a symmetrical triangle or a trading range below all three moving averages can produce equally explosive results.

Here's how it works:

1. Enter short on the first break below the neckline of the head-and-shoulders pattern. You can alternately use put options to enter the market. I like to take this route because the maximum gain on this type of trade usually occurs after at least two trading days.

2. Use a tight stop (maybe 1/2 to 1 point at the most). This is a high-probability pattern; if the trade doesn't go my way immediately, I get out. If I get stopped out, I reenter if the stock breaks the neckline again.

Figure 2.3 shows an example of a trade I took in SLB. The stock was definitely in a slide, having traded for months below its 50- and 200-day moving averages. The head-and-shoulders pattern developed in October and November, essentially offering a pause in the downtrend and an opportunity to jump on board should the free fall continue. SLB broke below the neckline on November 27, 1998, and I got short at 49 1/4 (I placed an initial stop at 50 1/16). SLB then traded down to 40 1/16 over the next six days. Institutions, who might have been fooled into thinking the market might have been forming a bottom around the time of the

FIGURE 2.3

Devil's House: Schlumberger (SLB), Daily

Schlumberger Ltd-Daily 01/25/99 C=50.000 -1.500 O=51.500 H=51.500 L=49.938 V=2050900

head-and-shoulders pattern developed, bailed out of their positions for fear of sustaining any more damage. I covered my position at 41 11/16 on December 7 because the stock closed above the December 4 high of 41 5/8, a day on which it closed at the top of its range (and a reversal to the upside had started).

I've found trading isn't just about looking at chart patterns. You have to have an understanding of what's going on behind them. As an example, there were a few other telltale signs that told me it was time to get out of this trade. Volume had gotten very heavy and the market was showing support around 40, suggesting that maybe the company was buying back stock or some institutions were bottom fishing (or both). Also, at 40, SLB was down more than 50 percent from its November 1997 high; it was about time for some Wall Street research firm to start putting out a story about the stock's "value," how the upside potential was much greater than the downside risk, how "things can only get better," and so on.

This is an important point, and one I think many traders don't appreciate: Analysts get rated for timing—and what they say and do to boost their own ratings can affect prices. When a stock has dropped like the one in our example, an analyst can take a calculated gamble. He'll look like a genius if the stock does, in fact, rally at that moment. If it stays at the same level or declines more, he can always say his call was a little "early." If an institution eventually buys his story (and as a result, the stock), he will have been the first to put out the word and he and his firm will score points in the research ratings game.

CONCLUSION

The strategies I've outlined for you reflect the market realities I've come to appreciate over the course of my 25 years in the trading industry. I do what makes sense to me: I use simple price patterns that help me take advantage of situations in which the institutional activity is in my favor, complemented by tight risk control and money management that keeps my per trade risk small and my profit potential high.

CHAPTER 3

How I Trade Momentum Stocks

by Jeff Cooper

Jeff Cooper is a professional stock trader and author of three best-selling books on short-term stock trading strategies: Hit & Run Trading I, Hit & Run Trading II, *and* The 5-Day Momentum Method. *Mr. Cooper's career in the markets began in 1981, when he worked at Drexel Burnham Lambert. He discovered a love for the financial markets and a fascination with what made them move. He started trading for his own account in 1983 and dedicated himself exclusively to his private trading in 1986. Based in Malibu, California, Mr. Cooper has been a successful trader ever since.*

I have made my living as a professional trader for more than 15 years. During this time I have methodically developed a successful trading approach based upon a core set of commonsense (but often overlooked) market principles. One of the things I've noticed over the years is that most investors completely ignore shorter-term stock trading opportunities, specifically those offered by reactions within long-term trends—even though these are some of the lowest-risk, highest-potential situations they could ever hope to find.

When stocks run up sharply, they tend to pullback for 3 to 10 days as profit-takers lock in their gains. After this so-called resting period, such stocks often continue their up trends. I have learned that one of the best ways to trade stocks is to identify strongly trending companies that have pulled back and are poised to resume their longer-term move.

TRADING PULLBACKS TO JUMP ON TRENDS: 1-2-3-4s

One of my favorite methods of capitalizing on the tendency of trending markets to pull back is called "1-2-3-4s" because the setup takes four days to complete. Days 1, 2, and 3 form a countertrend move in a strongly trending market. Day 4 is when you enter your trade. I like to climb aboard these stocks as the move begins, and I stay with them for as short as a few hours to as long as a few days. These are the rules:

1. Identify a strongly trending stock. This can be done by using the Relative Strength rankings on the

TRADEHARD.COM site or in *Investors Business Daily*. Ideally, you want to trade stocks with RS rankings of 95 or above.

2. Wait for the stock to make a three-day pullback, especially following a short-term high. This means that after making a short-term high, the stock makes three consecutive lower lows, or a combination of lower lows and inside days. (Inside days are days for which the high is less than or equal to the previous day's high and the low is greater than or equal to the previous day's low).

As I've noted, three-day pullbacks are a common phenomenon in strongly trending stocks. The important question is, how should you enter the market in these situations? For up-trending markets, enter long on Day 4, 1/16 of a point above the Day-3 high.

After I enter a position, I always protect myself with a stop order near the Day-3 low. For example, if the Day-3 high is 42 1/4 and the low is 41 1/2, buy the stock on Day 4 at 42 5/16 (41 1/2 plus 1/16) and place a good-till-canceled (GTC) stop order near 41 1/2. This is what I do to help minimize my losses if the position goes against me. Pullbacks offer great trading opportunities, but if you don't use proper risk control, the best entry technique in the world won't do you any good.

Let's look at a complete example of the 1-2-3-4 strategy. Figure 3.1 shows a strong rally in Quality Foods in early 1998. The stock had an RS reading of 97 in mid-February, fulfilling our requirement for a stock with an RS level of 95 or

FIGURE 3.1

1-2-3-4 Buy Setup: Quality Foods, Daily

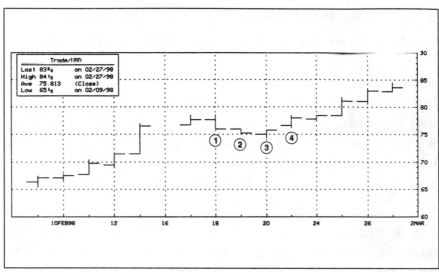

Source: Bloomberg LP.

above (which denotes a strongly uptrending stock). The setup began after the market made a new high on February 17, 1998.

Day 1. First lower low after the new high.

Day 2. Second lower low.

Day 3. Third lower low.

Day 4. Buy one tick (1/16) above the Day-3 high of 75 3/4. Place a protective stop near the Day-3 low of 74 3/8.

As the chart shows, the stock jumped more than $8 over the next four days.

Using 1-2-3-4s to Trade Both Sides of the Market

Another attractive facet of 1-2-3-4s is that they are great for shorting the stock market—something every successful trader must know how to do. From 1982 through 1998 the stock market rose a majority of the time, creating a generation of "buy only" equity traders and investors conditioned into believing this was the way the market worked and always would. Unfortunately, while many of these long-side-only traders may have profited during this unusually long bull run, they will get decimated in a bear market. This is not a prediction, it is a guarantee.

I've learned firsthand that you need strategies that are profitable in declining markets as well as rising ones to successfully trade stocks in the long run. This means shorting stocks. For example, 1-2-3-4s and other pullback strategies buy strong stocks after they make minor retracements. You can simply invert this concept to short weak stocks. All you do is identify imploding (declining) stocks and wait for them to rally a few days. When they begin to resume their longer-term downtrend, they become solid short-selling candidates.

Figure 3.2 shows a 1-2-3-4 setup for the short side of the market in Circuit City. You can identify a downtrend by making sure prices are under both their 50- and 20-day moving averages. The setup rules mirror those in uptrending markets. In these situations, though, you wait for three higher highs (or a combination of higher highs and inside days) before entering short. After the new low on August 14, 1998, the trade developed as follows:

FIGURE 3.2

1-2-3-4 Sell Setup: Circuit City (CC), Daily

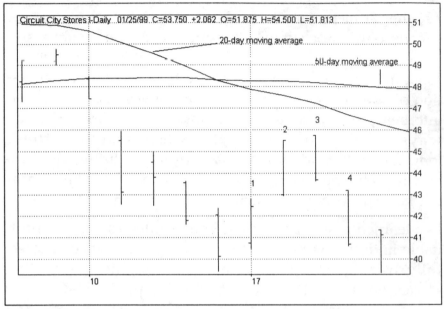

Source: Omega Research, Inc.

Day 1. First higher high off the new low.

Day 2. Second higher high.

Day 3. Third higher high.

Day 4. Sell short one tick below the Day 3 low. Place a protective stop near the Day 3 high. The stock closes 1 7/16 points below our entry level.

There are several other pullback strategies discussed throughout the book that give you plenty of options for taking advantage of this market characteristic. As always, discipline and risk control will make or break a trading approach. Remember to keep your stops tight and learn to lock in profits when possible.

You can find the names of the stocks with the best pull-backs every day in the Stock Traders section of TRADEHARD.COM.

STEPPING IN FRONT OF SIZE™—A SUPERIOR WAY TO DAY TRADE

In *Hit and Run Trading*, I introduced a day-trading strategy I call "Stepping In Front Of Size." It's a great way to play off the dynamics of institutions or other larger traders chasing a limited number of shares of a particular stock. Here's how it works:

1. The stock must have a relative strength (RS) reading of 95 or higher. (A high ADX reading— with the +DI greater the –DI reading—also can be used to identify trending stocks.) This strategy is only for stocks traded on the New York Stock Exchange (NYSE) or the American Stock Exchange (ASE).

2. The average daily volume for the stock should be under 200,000 shares a day. *The lower the volume, the more money you will make with this strategy.*

3. The stock *must* be trading higher for the day. This strategy does not work for stocks down on the day.

4. Most importantly, the buyers must show they are impatient or there must be more than one institution trading this strategy. How do you know

if this is the case? By looking for *two consecutive higher bid prices where there is size to buy* ("size," in this case, means 5,000 shares or more).

For example, you want to see a market with 5,000 shares bid at 52 and 1,000 offered at 52 1/4. Then, look for the bid to go to 52 1/8 or 52 1/4 with 5,000 shares to buy again. This means someone is desperate to buy stock.

5. Next, if the market goes to 52 1/8 bid (with 5,000 to buy) and 52 3/8 offer, you will buy the offer. The only time you should ignore this higher bid is when 5,000 or more shares are offered just above it. This means there may be a seller who can accommodate the large buyer, which would eliminate the chance of a big jump occurring in the stock.

6. Place a protective stop 1/16th point under the price of the original 5,000 share bid (52 in this case).

7. Where to take profits is very subjective. Many times, if there is size on the offer side or if you see the institution has been filled, you will automatically take profits.

Why does this strategy work so well? Because impatient institutional buyers bid up for the stock in an effort to complete their purchase as quickly as possible. When two or three institutions are buying at the same time, it creates a buying frenzy that drives prices to the moon. By risking (usually) no more than 3/8 to 1/2 point, you can often lock in two- to four-point gains.

Figure 3.3 shows Sun International Hotels, averaging approximately 66,000 shares per day in volume. At the time of

FIGURE 3.3
Stepping In Front Of Size: Sun International Hotels, Daily

```
 Page                                                        DG28 Equity Q R M
 Screen printed.
                         M A R K E T / T R A D E   R E C A P              Page 3
      Time  :       Min Vol   100        Volumes scaled by 100
      Date  7/1  Price Range          to
 SUN INTL HOTELS LTD      (SIH    US)              PRICE 48     N     $
 Time  E   Bid/Trd/Ask  E   Size   Cond Time  E   Bid/Trd/Ask  E   Size   Cond
 13:20 N   49³₈/49³₄    N   50x1        13:13 N   49/49¹₈      N   10x5
 13:20 N   49³₈/49³₄    B   50x1        13:13 N   49/49¹ₕ      N   5x5
 13:20 N   ↑49⁵₈            1           13:11 N   48³₄/49¹₈    N   50x5
 13:19 N   49³₈/49⁵₈    N   50x1        13:00 N   48⁵₈/49      N   50x5   ②
 13:18 N   49¹₂            10           13:00 N   48⁷₈             5
 13:18 N   49¹₂             5           13:00 N   ↑48⁷₈            5
 13:17 N   49³₈/49³₄    N   50x5        12:38 N   48¹₂/48⁷₈    N   50x5   ①
 13:17 N   49³₈/49⁵₈    B   50x1        12:24 N   ↓48⁵₈           34
 13:17 N   49¹₂            10           12:24 N   48¹₂/48⁷₈    N   10x5
 13:17 N   ↑49¹₂            5           10:54 N   48⁵₈/49      N   20x5
 13:15 N   49¹₄            10           10:54 N   48¹₂/49¹₈    N   5x5
 13:15 N   49¹₈/49¹₂    N   50x5        10:54 N   ↑48⁷₈           11
 13:15 N   ↑49¹₄            5           10:54 N   48¹₂/49      B   5x1
 13:14 N   49/49³₈      N   50x5        10:41 N   48¹₂/48⁷ₓ    N   5x5
 13:13 N   49¹₈             5           10:41 N   ↑48³₄            2
 13:14 N   49/49¹₄      B   50x1        10:39 N   48³₈/48³₄    N   5x5
 13:13 N   49¹₈             5           10:39 N   ↓48¹₂            6
 13:13 N   ↑49¹₈            5           10:29 N   ↑48³₄            1
```

Source: Bloomberg LP.

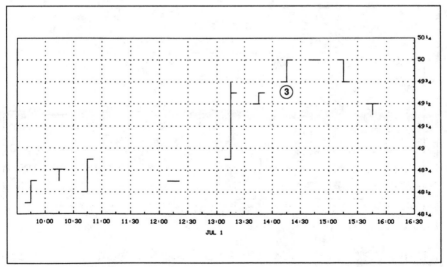

Source: Bloomberg LP.

FIGURE 3.4
Stepping In Front Of Size: Sturm Ruger, Daily

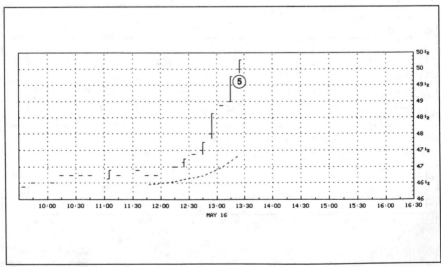

```
  Page                                                    DG26 Equity Q R M
  Screen printed.        M A R K E T / T R A D E  R E C A P             Page 3
     Time ░░.░    Min Vol   100      Volumes scaled by 100
     Date  5/16  Price Range ░░░░░ to ░░░░░
  STURM RUGER & CO INC      (RGR   US)              PRICE 50     N   $
 │Time  E  Bid/Trd/Ask  E   Size   Cond│Time  E  Bid/Trd/Ask  E   Size    Cond│
  12:54 N   48¹₂             3            12:50 N    48              5
  12:54 N  ↓48¹₂             3            12:50 N   ↑48              5
  12:54 T  ↑48⁵₈             5            12:50 N  47³₄/48       N  100x5
  12:54 N  ↑48¹₂             6            12:50 N  47³₄/47⁷₈     T  100x5      OLDE
  12:53 N  48¹₄/48¹₂   N  250x5 (4)       12:50 N  47³₄/47³₄     T  100x5 (1)  OLDE
  12:53 N   48¹₄             5            12:49 N  47³₈/47³₄     T   5x5        OLDE
  12:53 N  48¹₈/48¹₂   N  100x5           12:49 N  ↑47³₄             5
  12:53 N  48¹₈/48¹₂   T  100x5      OLDE 12:48 M  ↓47³₈             1
  12:53 N  48¹₈/48¹₄   X  100x1 (3)       12:46 M   47¹₂             2
  12:53 N   48¹₄             5            12:46 N  47³₈/47³₄     T   5x5        OLDE
  12:53 N   48¹₄             5            12:46 N  47³₈/47¹₂     X   5x1
  12:52 N  ↑48¹₄            12            12:46 M   47¹₂             8
  12:50 N  48/48¹₄     N  250x5           12:46 N  47³₈/47¹₂     X   8x1
  12:50 N  48/48¹₄     T  250x5      OLDE 12:46 N   47¹₂            10
  12:50 N  48/48¹₈     P  250x1           12:46 M   47¹₂             8
  12:50 M  ↓47⁷₈             1            12:46 N   47¹₂            10
  12:50 N  48/48       X  250x1 (2)       12:46 N  ↑47¹₂             4
  12:50 N   48               5            12:34 M  47³₈/47¹₂     N   8x5
```

Source: Bloomberg LP.

Source: Bloomberg LP.

this trade, the stock was trending up: It had an ADX reading greater than 30 and the +DI was greater than the -DI. At 12:38 p.m. 5000 shares are bid at 48 1/2 (1). At 1:00 p.m., the buyer raises his bid to 48 5/8, triggering a buy signal (2). The stock immediately takes off, hitting 50 before the trading session is over (3).

Figure 3.4, Sturm Ruger, gives another example. The stock was enjoying a nice upswing in spring 1996, and institutions were dying to get in on the action. At 12:50 p.m., a buyer bids 47 3/4 on 10,000 shares (1). A few seconds later, the bid is raised (probably by a second buyer) to 48, triggering our buy signal (2). The bid gets raised again and again (3 and 4), and the stock shoots up to 50 1/4 before the dueling buyers get their stock (5).

CONCLUSION

Trading pullbacks in strongly trending stocks (1-2-3-4s) and taking advantage of institutional trading patterns in thin markets (Stepping in Front of Size) are two of the best commonsense short-term strategies I know. They are based on my observations—taken from 15 years in the markets—of the kind of forces that really move markets. They reflect the principles of any good stock trading strategy: They trade with the momentum of the market; they limit risk; they take into account the realities of market dynamics; and they offer (in the case of 1-2-3-4s) the opportunity to trade both sides of the market.

CHAPTER 4

How I Use Historical Volatility to Identify Market Explosions

by Larry Connors

Laurence Connors is a professional trader and the author of Investment Secrets of a Hedge Fund Manager, Street Smarts *(with Linda Raschke), and* Connors on Advanced Trading Strategies, *all best-selling financial markets books.*

Mr. Connors is also founder and Chief Executive Officer of the trading information companies M. Gordon Publishing Group and TRADEHARD.COM, as well as Connors, Bassett & Associates, a money management firm. He founded these companies after a successful career with Donaldson, Lufkin & Jenrette and Merrill Lynch.

As a short-term trader, I try to avoid being in markets that are not moving. Back in the early 1990s, I developed a method using historical volatility that allows me to pinpoint when markets are likely to experience larger than normal short-term moves.

The academic world proved more than four decades ago that all market volatility is mean reverting. What that means in the real world is that periods of low volatility are usually followed by periods of high volatility, and periods of high volatility are usually followed by periods of low volatility.

How do we as traders exploit this inherent market characteristic? With historical volatility (HV), which is the standard deviation of day-to-day logarithmic price changes expressed as an annualized percentage. (Don't worry about understanding the math behind historical volatility; applying the concept in the markets is straightforward.) When a shorter-term historical volatility calculation is one-half or less of a longer-term volatility calculation, explosive market moves often follow as volatility reverts to its mean.

I have found the two best periods to compare are the 6-day HV reading versus the 100-day HV reading (6/100) and the 10-day HV versus the 100-day reading (10/100). For example, if the 6-day HV reading is 15 percent and the 100-day HV reading is 45 percent, the shorter calculation (6 days) is .33 of the longer calculation (100 days). Because this is one-half or less of the longer period, it's highly likely a large move is imminent. (What this *doesn't* tell us is the direction of the move. It simply indicates a large move is likely).

Figures 4.1 and 4.2 provide examples of how this approach works in specific market situations. Both charts show price with ratios of short-term and long-term volatility, as described above. The horizontal lines in the volatility series mark the 50 percent level; when the volatility ratio moves below this line, short-term volatility is half or less of the long-term volatility and the market is setting up for a big move.

In Figure 4.1, the short-term volatility drops below half of the long-term volatility in the T-bond market on September 10 (day 1). After moving slightly lower the next day (day 2), the market explodes to the upside on September 12 (day 3), and moves three points higher over the next two trading days.

In Figure 4.2, the volatility ratio first drops below 50 percent on July 16 in the S&P 500 futures. Two days later, the market breaks to the downside (notice the accompanying surge in volatility that day as well), the beginning of a more than 100-point drop in the S&Ps.

Short-term breakout techniques offer an effective method to establish positions based on these low-volatility setups. We've found that fading the initial breakout move and trading in the direction of the reversal is a good way to avoid multiple repeated false signals that can occur at such explosive junctures. As always, risk control is key. Using a money management approach like the "2-for-1" method (see Chapter 9) will help minimize your risk and maximize your profitability.

There are additional ways to trade with this historical volatility information. For example, I have found the longer a

FIGURE 4.1

Explosion Out of a Low-Volatility Situation:
December 98 T-Bond Futures, Daily

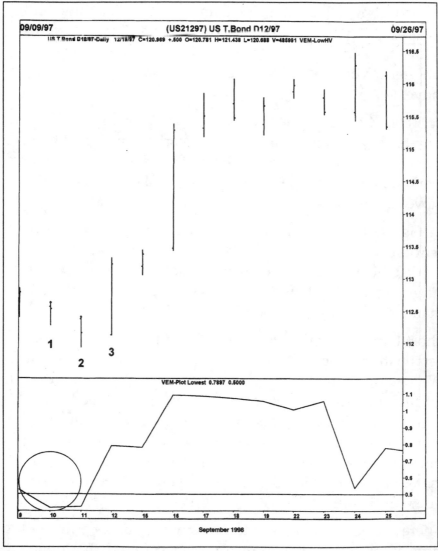

Source: Omega Research, Inc.

FIGURE 4.2

Explosion Out of a Low-Volatility Situation:
September 98 S&P 500 Futures, Daily

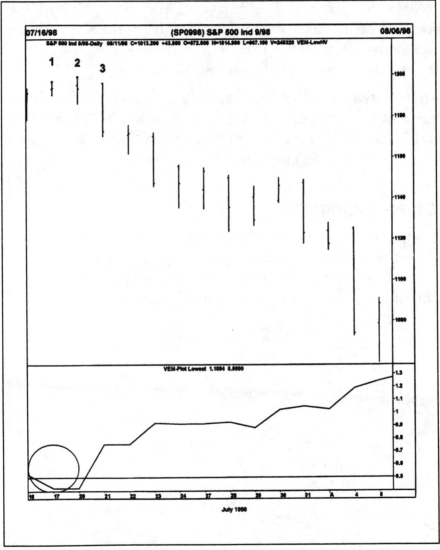

Source: Omega Research, Inc.

market stays under the 50 percent level, the bigger the move will be when it finally explodes. Earthquakes provide a useful analogy: The longer the time between tremors, the greater the pressure buildup, and the more violent the eventual earthquake. When you identify markets with readings under 50 percent for three, four, five or more days, you can rest assured the move will be substantial.

Another way I use these readings is to look for multiple signals. If a stock or future has both a low 6/100 reading and a low 10/100 reading the same day, it is likely that a large move will develop almost immediately.

CONCLUSION

Comparing short-term volatility to longer-term volatility is a solid method to identify pending market moves. This method exploits inherent market features and allows you to pinpoint which markets you should focus on.

CHAPTER 5

The Key to Capturing Profits in the Option Markets

by Robert Pisani, Ph.D.

Robert Pisani received a Ph.D. in statistics from the University of California at Berkeley in 1971. He subsequently joined the faculty at Berkeley, conducting extensive research on the securities and options markets. (He has also coauthored a college statistics text-book that has been a top-seller for over 20 years.)

His research on the markets led to the development of sophisticated mathematical options models and trading strategies that, unfortunately, could only be traded "on paper" because organized options markets were non-existent at the time. That all changed in 1975 when listed options first became available for trading on the Chicago Board Options Exchange (CBOE) and the Pacific Coast Stock Exchange (PSE).

Taking advantage of the opportunity to apply his strategies in real markets, Pisani founded a market maker firm, Galton-Gauss Securities, that traded on the CBOE and the PSE with the express purpose of "achieving extraordinary gains." Using Pisani's proprietary option trading models, Galton-Gauss did just that for the next half-dozen years.

Pisani has continued to trade as well as research and test successful options trading models. He also is a visiting scholar at the University of California at Berkeley.

I started trading options nearly 25 years ago when the listed options exchanges first opened their doors. Option trading was a wide-open field then, and the option models and trading strategies I'd designed using my background as a statistician proved to be quite effective at exploiting the pricing discrepancies that were prevalent in those early years. However, as these ideas spread out among the larger trading community over the next few years (and as the options markets evolved), they lost some of the edge that had made them so profitable, and I had to look to other techniques.

The option markets *can* be confusing to newcomers, and they certainly have become much more competitive over the last two decades, but finding an edge still hinges on a few basic principles. I've learned from experience that the key to making profits in options is to buy undervalued options and sell overvalued options; that's no secret. What remains is to find the best way to measure when options are exceptionally underpriced or exceptionally overpriced, and then to use the trading strategies that allow you to exploit these situations most effectively.

IMPLIED VERSUS HISTORICAL VOLATILITY

An excellent way to determine whether an option price is unusually low or high is to compare the current implied volatility to the historical volatility. Historical volatility is simply the standard deviation of percentage price changes over a certain recent time period, expressed as an annualized percentage. Implied volatility gets its name from the fact that it is the volatility being "implied" by the price of an option using a theoretical model, typically the Black–Scholes model. The greater the volatility of the underlying, the greater the theoretical value of the option. The volatility that causes the theoretical value to be equal to the market price of the option is the implied volatility.

When you compare implied volatility to longer-term (say, 100-day) historical volatility, you are essentially comparing the current market estimate of future volatility to the recent average volatility of the underlying. **When implied volatility is very low compared to historical volatility, options tend to be underpriced, making them excellent candidates for purchases. When implied volatility is very high com-**

pared to historical volatility, options tend to be over-priced, making them excellent candidates for sales.

UNDERPRICED AND OVERPRICED OPTIONS

Let's look at some of these volatility figures and how they can point to potential option trading strategies. Table 5.1 shows a list of stocks with the degree of under-pricing (referred to as the "Ratio") for their options in the right-hand column. A ratio of 1.0 would mean the option is priced correctly relative to its 100-day historical volatility. For example, SEG has a Ratio of .89. This means the implied volatility of SEG options is, on average, about 89 percent of the 100-day historical volatility—that is, SEG options are, roughly speaking, selling for about 89 percent of their value. In this list, CCI's options are the most underpriced, trading for about 76 percent of their value relative to the historical volatility CCI.

If you simply want to buy options, these are the greatest bargains, meaning they have the lowest price relative to value. They give you the best edge for option purchases, long backspreads, long straddles, and long strangles. (These strategies are discussed in the following section.). **In practice, options become potentially attractive candidates for these strategies when they are at, or below the .70 level, and they are exceptionally underpriced only when they reach, or drop below, the .50 level.**

The same technique can be used to identify inflated option premiums. Table 5.2 shows a list of stocks with the degree

TABLE 5.1

Underpriced Options: Stocks with Implied Volatility/Historical
Volatility Ratios Less Than 1.00

Stock	Ratio
SEG	.89
BLS	.86
RN	.85
F	.82
SWY	.81
BEL	.80
DAI	.80
BGEN	.79
CQ	.78
GTE	.78
CCI	.76

of overpricing for their options in the right-hand column.
Again, a ratio of 1.00 reflects options that are fairly priced
in terms of the 100-day historical volatility. On this list,
WFC's options are the most overpriced relative to its
100-day historical volatility; they are, on average, priced
around 85 percent higher than their value relative to historical volatility. The 1.85 ratio means the implied volatility of WFC options is, on average, 1.85 times WFC's
100-day historical volatility.

TABLE 5.2

Overpriced Options: Stocks with Implied Volatility/Historical
Volatility Ratios Greater Than 1.00

Stock	Ratio
WFC	1.85
ABI	1.82
WDC	1.75
AMP	1.71
CPWR	1.70
QCOM	1.68
BT	1.55
ABTX	1.51
CIEN	1.49
DKB	1.48

If you are interested in selling options, these offer the highest premiums relative to value. They would give you the best edge for outright sales, covered writes, short straddles, and short strangles. **In practice, options become potentially attractive candidates for these strategies when they are at or above the 1.40 level.**

One thing you always have to keep in mind is that options may be overpriced for a reason related to future news. There may be a takeover in the works, a report of unusual earnings may soon be released, or there may be other not-yet-public news that will dramatically affect the price of a stock or future, which may justify higher option premiums. In these cases, the historical volatility will not be a good estimate of the volatility between now and expiration, and the values derived from it will be incorrect. Whenever you sell an option, alone or as part of a spread, it is important to keep these possibilities in mind.

The TRADEHARD.COM site provides daily updates of overpriced and underpriced OEX, stock, and futures options through the Underpriced Explosion Lists and the Overpriced Implosion Lists.

OPTION STRATEGIES

Professional option traders usually trade spreads, which are combinations of options that offer greater flexibility and better risk/reward characteristics than outright purchases or sales. Straddles, strangles, backspreads, and covered writes are some of the strategies you can use to capitalize on the kind of overpriced or underpriced options found on the TRADEHARD.COM option lists.

Straddles and Strangles

A long option *straddle* consists of a long call and a long put with the same strike price and expiration date (at-the-money options are typically used). For example, with Amazon.com at 150, the following positions are long straddles:

1. Long one April 150 call, long one April 150 put.

2. Long one Jan 140 call, long one Jan 140 put.

The following position is a short straddle:

3. Short one April 160 call, short one April 160 put.

Long straddles are attractive for a few reasons. First, your risk is limited to what you pay for the options. Second, you can profit from big moves in the underlying market without having to be correct on the direction of the move. Third, your potential profit is theoretically unlimited. And, if the market moves enough to exceed the cost of the straddle, you make money. Figure 5.1 shows a profit profile for a long straddle.

Option *strangles* are like straddles except that instead of buying a call and a put with the same strike price (for a long strangle), you typically buy an out-of-the-money call with a strike price above the current underlying price and an out-of-the-money put with a strike price below the current underlying price. Like straddles, strangles allow you to profit regardless of the direction of a price move. Because both options are out-of-the-money, long strangles are cheaper than straddles, but they also have reduced profit potential. For example, with IBM at 150, the following positions are long strangles:

1. Long one April 160 call, long one April 140 put.

2. Long one Jan 160 call, long one Jan 130 put.

The following is a short strangle:

3. Short one April 160 call, short one April 140 put.

FIGURE 5.1

Long Straddle

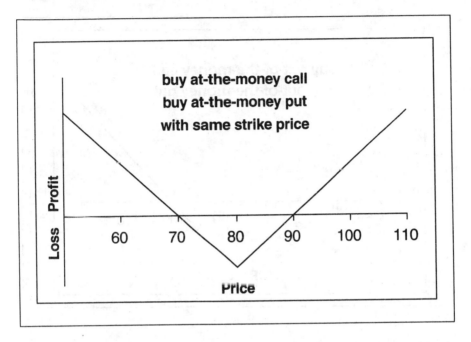

buy at-the-money call
buy at-the-money put
with same strike price

Figure 5.2 shows a profit profile for a long strangle. Long straddles and strangles are essentially ways to take advantage of lower-volatility situations in which options are cheaper and poised to jump in value when volatility explodes. They have the added bonus of flexibility and defined risk. Options on the Underpriced Explosion lists make good candidates for these trades.

When you sell a straddle or a strangle, the characteristics of the position and your goals on the trade are exactly the opposite: Because you are taking in option premium, you would naturally benefit from selling the most expensive op-

FIGURE 5.2
Long Strangle

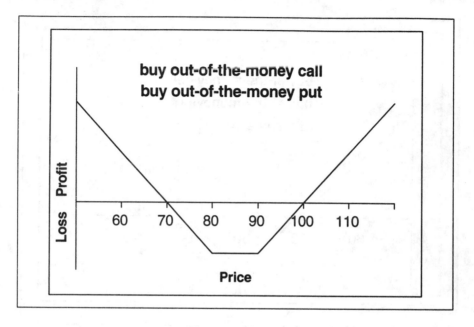

tions you can find and you would want volatility to decrease over the life of the position. The high-volatility options on the Overpriced Implosion Lists are excellent candidates for these trades.

Backspreads

A standard call *backspread* is long several at-the-money call options and short the underlying stock or future, or an in-the-money call option. Backspreads have limited loss and unlimited profit potential and are a favorite of many professional traders. Figure 5.3 shows the profit on a backspread at expiration.

FIGURE 5.3
Call Backspread

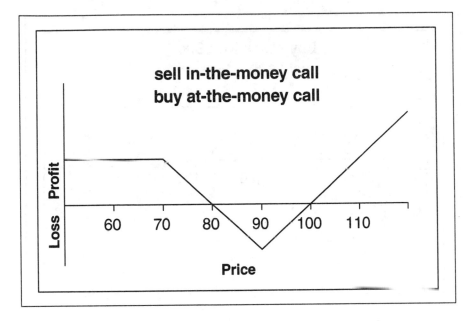

Backspreads can be constructed substituting an in-the-money option for the underlying stock or future, but this is a more sophisticated technique and should be undertaken only with the assistance of software that can tell you whether the options you are purchasing and selling are underpriced or overpriced (and by how much).

Covered Writes

If you already own 100 shares of a stock, you can, of course, safely sell an option against that stock because if the option is exercised you will merely have to deliver your stock to

FIGURE 5.4
Covered Write

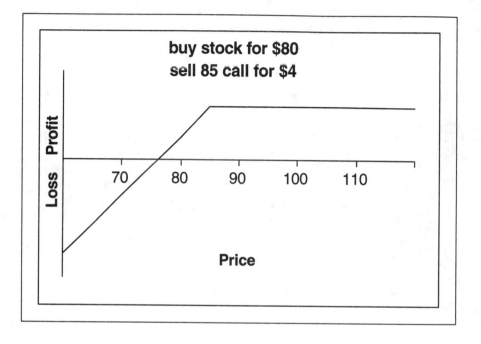

the option owner. Whether the call is exercised or not, the premium you collect for selling the call is yours to keep. This position, long the underlying and short one call, is called a covered write. If you see a call option trading at a high premium and want to sell it but do not already own the stock, you can purchase the stock and simultaneously sell the call. Some traders use this strategy to produce regular income. The trick, of course, is to choose the options you sell carefully, making certain they are overpriced. These are examples of covered writes with IBM trading at 150:

1. Long 100 shares IBM, short one April 160 call.

2. Long 100 shares IBM, short one Jan 170 call.

Figure 5.4 shows the profit profile for a covered write in which a stock is purchased at $80 and an 85 call is sold for $4.

CONCLUSION

Professional option traders use strategies that allow them to sell overpriced options and buy underpriced options using implied volatility. Determining when implied volatility is very low or very high compared to historical volatility is the easiest way I know to identify underpriced and overpriced options. Straddles, strangles, backspreads, and covered writes are a few of the strategies you can use to capitalize on this key aspect of option pricing and market behavior.

Chapter 6

My Three Favorite Trend Strategies

by Dave Landry

Dave Landry is president of Sentive Trading, a money management and research firm, and director of research for TRADEHARD.COM. Mr. Landry, who holds a BS in computer science as well as an MBA, entered the trading industry after a successful career in management information systems. Always fascinated by trading, in 1988 he embarked upon an in-depth analysis of the financial markets using technical and statistical analysis. In 1995 he decided to devote himself full time to the markets, and in 1996 he became a Commodity Trading Advisor (CTA) and founded Sentive Trading.

Mr. Landry's trading articles have been published in Technical Analysis of Stocks and Commodities *magazine, and he has authored a number of trading system manuals, including the 2/20 EMA Breakout System. His research has been referenced in several books, including* Connors On Advanced Trading Strategies *and* Beginners Guide to Computerized Trading.

Once I decided to become a professional trader, I quickly discovered the gap between the "theories" I'd read in many books and magazines and the realities of making a living in the markets. Although it might have sounded easy enough, you couldn't, for example, simply buy a market because it was going up. In the same vein, I realized that trying to pick tops and bottoms was a sure way to get killed.

One basic trading rule that *did* made sense to me, though, was to trade with the trend. To succeed, I knew I'd have to find patterns that exploited this fundamental market characteristic while allowing me to capture short-term market moves with minimal risk. The three trend-following strategies I'll share with you—Running Cups and Handles, Trend Knockouts, and Trend Pivot Pullbacks—are the techniques I developed to help me achieve this goal. But before we discuss these strategies, let's look at the dynamics of price trends to better understand how these strategies capitalize on them.

HOW TRENDS ARE CREATED

There's nothing really mysterious about price trends. When buyers begin to bid up a market, it catches the attention of other potential buyers. These traders don't want to be left behind, so they, too, begin buying, which in turn attracts even more longs. This buying momentum begets more buying momentum, as greed pushes an increasing number of traders into the market. It's a self-reinforcing process.

Obviously, trends cannot last forever, but they often continue for much longer than many people expect, making top and bottom picking difficult, if not impossible. Trending markets repeatedly pause or pull back, leading traders to think the trend has ended—only to be trapped when the market continues in its previous direction. As a result, it's much more profitable (and easier) to go with the flow—with the trend—than it is to fight the market.

I'm not saying you should blindly buy or sell a market just because it is trending. You never know when what appears to be a correction may turn out to be the end of the original move and vice versa. You have to pick your points wisely. I have found it's best to identify a correction in a trending market and then wait for the market to pivot back in the direction of the original trend. This allows profit-taking to occur and for the "weak hands" to be shaken out of the market during the pullback. (Weak hands, or "fast money," are those smaller traders with very little staying power, as opposed to large institutions or commercial interests; they are easily shaken out the markets.) Once these players are gone, the path is cleared for the market to resume its underlying trend.

The strategies I use identify strongly trending markets that have corrected or shaken out the weak hands (or both). I enter my trades only after price has pivoted back into the direction of the longer-term trend to ensure I'm not on the wrong side of the market. Also, because the correction has already occurred and the market has turned back in the direction of the original trend, I can use a tighter protective stop to reduce my risk.

RUNNING CUP-AND-HANDLE PATTERN

The cup-and-handle pattern was popularized by William O'Neil. In most cases, the "cup" is created when a market sells off and then forms a rounded bottom. The market then rallies slightly and pulls back, forming the "handle," which is often followed by an upside reversal. Sometimes, though, the underlying trend is so strong the market forms a cup in the midst of a rally, that is, while the market is still "running" (hence the name). This less-common form of the pattern often precedes particularly substantial moves because the cup-and-handle pattern represents a pullback of sorts within a strong, already established trend—increasing the likelihood that resumption of the trend, when it occurs, will be that much more forceful. In essence, you have the advantage of a bottom formation combined with an uptrend—two bullish patterns working together.

Here's the setup:

1. The stock must be trading above its 50-day moving average, defining an uptrend.

FIGURE 6.1

Running Cup-and-Handle Pattern: Dell Computer (DELL), Daily

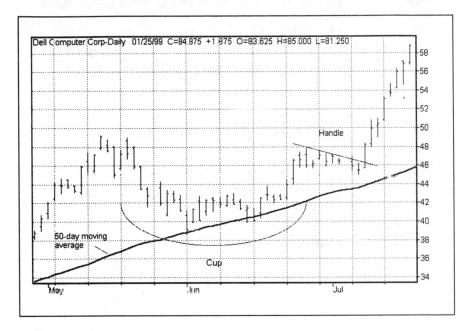

2. A rounded sell-off should ensue that forms a "cup" at or above the 50-day moving average.

3. The market should pull back to form the handle.

4. Go long when the stock resumes its uptrend out of the handle.

Figure 6.1 shows how on May 13, 1998, Dell was in a strong uptrend, trading well above its 50-day moving average. It subsequently sold off and formed a cup just at the level of the moving average. Coming out of the cup, it drifted lower, forming a handle. Finally, on July 8, 1998, it exploded out of the handle, triggering our buy order. The market gained nearly 30 percent over the next eight days.

By trading a cup-and-handle pattern that forms within an existing trend, you get the best of both worlds: a bottom formation and momentum automatically on your side.

TREND KNOCKOUTS (TKOs)

While it's a good idea to trade in the direction of the trend, I've learned you're much better off waiting until the weak hands are knocked out of the market before entering yourself. The problem is that you never know when these traders are going to dump their positions and take you out with them. Trend Knockouts (TKOs) identify strong trends from which the weak hands have already been knocked out. By placing your order above the market, you have the potential to capture profits as the trend resumes.

For this technique, I use the ADX to identify strongly moving markets and then use a short-term pullback signal to get in on the trend. The ADX was developed by Welles Wilder and outlined in his book *New Concepts in Technical Trading Systems* (1978, Trend Research). The formula is quite lengthy, but the indicator essentially measures up price moves and down price moves from day to day ("Directional Movement," expressed as +DM for up movement and –DM for down movement). The ADX averages these calculations over a certain number of days, measuring trend strength but not direction; the stronger the trend—up or down—the higher the ADX reading. (A quick look at the example below will show the relationship between the ADX and trend.)

These are the TKO buy rules (reverse for sells):

1. Identify a strongly trending market as measured by a 14-period ADX reading greater than 25 (the higher the better) and a +DMI reading greater than the –DMI reading. (+DMI and –DMI are averages of the up and down directional movement calculations described earlier. They are often shown as plotted as separate lines along with the ADX.) Alternately, for stocks, you can use issues with relative strength readings of 98 or 99.

2. Today's low must trade below the low of the two prior bars.

3. If rules 1 and 2 are met, go long tomorrow 1/8 of a point (for stocks) or one tick (for futures) above today's high.

4. Exit in one to three days, using a trailing stop to protect profits.

Here's a trade in the T-bond futures that shows how TKOs work. In Figure 6.2, on September 28, 1998, the 14-period ADX reading in the December 1998 T-bond futures was 56.77 and the +DMI was greater than the –DMI (1), which tells me I'm working with a strong uptrend. Bonds then traded below the lowest low of the prior two bars (2)—the pullback I look for before I enter the market. I place a buy stop one tick above the current high (130-05) for execution the next day (3). Bonds gap open, filling the order at 130-12.

FIGURE 6.2

TKO: December 1998 T-Bond Futures, Daily

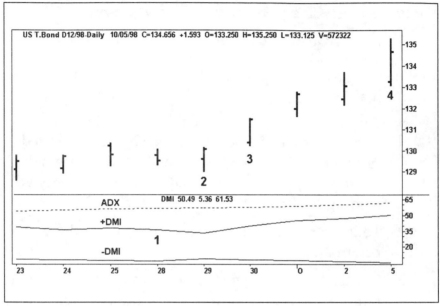

US T.Bond D12/98-Daily 10/05/98 C=134.656 +1.593 O=133.250 H=135.250 L=133.125 V=572322

Source: Omega Research, Inc.

The market proceeds to trade nearly five points higher over the next three days (4).

TREND PIVOT PULLBACKS (FALSE RALLY PULLBACKS)

Pullbacks offer the best opportunities to get on board existing trends, but many traders make the mistake of entering too early because they want to get a jump on the market. Unfortunately, these anxious traders will quickly get shaken out of the market if the correction isn't finished. Once these new traders (along with the profit-takers) are out of the market, the trend is free to resume its course.

The Trend Pivot Pullback strategy uses two reference points to trigger trades (I'll describe these in terms of an up-trending market): a new high and a "pivot" high, which is a high with a lower high on both sides. For example, if IBM makes highs of 99 on Monday, 100 on Tuesday, and 98 on Wednesday, then Tuesday would be a pivot high because both Monday's and Wednesday's highs were lower than Tuesday's.

Trend Pivots go long after a market has begun a correction and then made a false move to the upside (the pivot high). A correction here is defined as a sell-off consisting of at least two (but no more than six) lower highs following a new 60-day high. Once this correction has begun (after at least two lower highs), I wait for the market to make a pivot high. In other words, after making the 60-day high, the market begins to sell off, has a one-day rally, then resumes its sell-off. This one-day rally attracts the "fast money" and the subsequent sell-off quickly shakes them out. I enter long when the market moves above the pivot high.

Let's look at the specific rules and an example. These are the buy rules (reverse for sells):

1. The market must make a two-month (60-day) high.

2. The market must subsequently make at least two, but no more than six, lower highs.

FIGURE 6.3

Trend Pivot Pullback: Amazon.com (AMZN), Daily

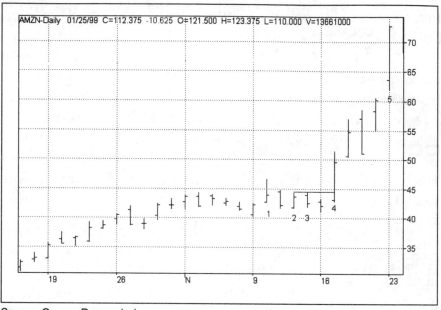

AMZN-Daily 01/25/99 C=112.375 -10.625 O=121.500 H=123.375 L=110.000 V=13661000

Source: Omega Research, Inc.

3. The market must then stage a one-day rally (a high greater than the prior day's high) followed by a lower high. This is also known as a pivot high.

4. Buy 1/8th point of a point (for stocks) or one tick (for futures) above the pivot high. Allow yourself up to two days for the order to be filled.

Figure 6.3 shows an example. On November 10, 1998, Amazon.com (AMZN) makes a two-month high (1). It then makes two lower highs (2), followed by a pivot high on November 13, 1998 (a higher high than those of the preceding and succeeding days) (3). We go long 1/8th of a point above the pivot day high (4). Over the next four days, AMZN explodes to the upside (5).

Pivot highs (or lows) shake out the fast money that tends to buy too early in a correction, leaving the market free to resume its longer-term underlying trend. Trend Pivot Pullbacks position you in the market when you'll benefit most from this aspect of market behavior.

CONCLUSION

Trading with the trend involves much less risk than trying to fight the markets by picking tops or bottoms. The best approach to take is to wait for markets to pull back and to enter once they resume their trends. The strategies I've described for you here are designed to take advantage of this kind of price action and put you in synch with the underlying trend. And like all the other successful traders I know, I always use tight stops to minimize my risk on every trade. As a result, when I'm wrong, I don't have to worry that a trade will turn into an account-crushing loser—a big plus when you're trading trend-following strategies.

CHAPTER 7

How I Design and Test a Trading Approach

by Manuel Ochoa

Manuel Ochoa is a hedge fund manager who began researching and developing trading strategies and models while he was still a student at the University of Southern California, from which he received a BS in Finance in 1990. With the assistance of his professors and the university statistical laboratory, he was able to test and verify the validity of his trading ideas, which ultimately compelled him to pursue trading on a full-time basis.

Mr. Ochoa has enjoyed great success trading both his personal account and his hedge fund since launching his career immediately after graduating from college. He has been profiled as one of the hottest new traders in Futures *magazine, and one of his funds was ranked third by Mar Hedge for its performance in 1997. He also continues to develop trading systems, and portfolio diversification and risk management models.*

As a professional hedge fund manager, I've designed, tested, and analyzed dozens of trading models and systems. I've learned that there's a lot more to this process than simply running some price data through a software "trading genie" that will tell you when to buy and sell. Mechanical systems have advantages and disadvantages, and the process of developing a good idea and testing and evaluating system results is not a cut-and-dried issue. In reviewing the nature of mechanical trading systems, I'll explore the following areas:

- Reasons to trade with systems.
- How to prepare a system development effort.
- Goals and limitations of historical testing.
- What you can learn from system test results, using a case study of an actual system development campaign.

WHY USE SYSTEMS TO TRADE MARKETS?

Before going into specifics about designing trading systems, I should probably explain why you should use them at all. Many people in the academic and financial world doubt the effectiveness of mechanical systems, claiming markets are efficient and that any information is quickly reflected in the price of any stock or futures contract, rendering systems useless. However, some academics are beginning to find that markets are not as efficient as they previously thought, explaining why some traders have been able to consistently make money in the markets.

If you have a trading idea that captures a logical, repetitive aspect of market behavior, a properly designed and tested trading system can help you exploit it efficiently. System trading also allows you to be consistent and disciplined over long time periods. By consistent and disciplined, I am referring specifically to being able to cut losses on losing positions and ride out winning positions as long as possible. Like any other profession, success requires a business plan. And that is precisely what a trading system is—a business plan.

PREPARING FOR HISTORICAL TESTING

Before trading any system with real money, you have to test it on past market data. If a system has not made money in the past, common sense dictates it will probably not make any money in the future. Testing is a multilayered process. First, you must decide what software you will use for testing and how much (and what kind of) historical price data you'll need. Luckily, the Internet is an excellent source of up-to-date information for both data and software vendors.

For the most part, only futures traders need to think about the kind of data they should use for testing. Futures data comes in several formats, and the type you use can seriously impact your test results. Futures markets are composed of successive contracts that expire throughout the year. If you want to test your system on multiple years of data (which you should definitely do), you will have to decide whether to roll these contracts as they expire or use a continuous contract (see below), which links many individual contract months in a single, unbroken price series. Rolling your positions using individual futures contracts requires programming your system to repeatedly liquidate your position in one contract and establish it in the next as you move forward through your test (just as you would in actual trading). If you did not do this, you would have distortions caused by the natural price gaps that occur from one contract to the next. This can be a very tedious process, however, and it is actually unnecessary.

Continuous futures adjust prices to compensate for the gaps in individual contract data, so they also provide an accurate reflection of price movement over the course of any historical period. Also, continuous futures are easier to work with than individual contracts because there is only a single data series to input. The only compensation you must make when testing with continuous data is to account fully for commissions and slippage that would have occurred when positions were rolled from one contract month to the next. When you buy your data, just be sure you know what kind you are buying before you pay for it. Your vendor should be able to explain how they adjust prices for their continuous data and whether it is suitable for your testing needs.

Finally, if you are testing your system on historical stock or cash index data, you don't have to worry about these problems because there are no expiring contracts to deal with. (The only issue you should be aware of is the effect of stock splits on historical test results. Consult your data vendor regarding how the company handles splits in their price data and how you can adjust for it in your testing.)

CONSTRUCTING A REALISTIC TEST

Test results are only as good as the rules you use to conduct the tests. It's easy to make any system look good on past data; the goal is to get a realistic idea of the future potential of your system.

How much price data should you test your system on? The best answer is, as much as you can—within reason. You can use a few guidelines to estimate how much price data you'll need. First, long-term systems require longer data periods. If you have a system that only generates a handful of signals per year, it will take many years of test data to compile enough hypothetical trades to gauge its value. A shorter-term system won't necessarily require as long a test period, but there's never any point in skimping if you have the price data. Your goal is to test on enough price data that your system experiences a variety of market environments. If you only test on, say, two, three, or even five years of daily data, your results may be misleading. If, for example, a market was experiencing an extended trend during your limited time window, you might think your trend-following system was better than it really was or your countertrend system was worse than it really was. The longer the time period you test, the greater the chances your test results will not reflect limited or coincidental price behavior. A rough minimum for system testing might be 10 years of daily data for a longer-term system.

Another idea is to test your system on distinct price data sets and compare results between the tests. Comparable performance across all of them suggests your system is reliable. For example, if you have 20 years of data, you could test the system on the first 10 years of data, then conduct a new test on the next 5 years of data, then on the next 3 years of data, and finally, the last 2 years. You could also test the entire 20-year period.

You must also be sure to factor in appropriate commissions and slippage on all your test trades. (Slippage is the difference between your desired price and your actual fill price.) Some systems look great in hypothetical testing until you realize you forgot to account for costs for each of the 500 trades in your test period. If you know your commission rate, that's simple, but slippage is not as easy to calculate. If you've already traded, maybe you have a good idea of the slippage in the markets you're active in. The trick is to estimate on the high side, but not too high—you may rule out systems that might be profitable.

One final trap for novice system designers is over-optimizing ("fitting") their systems. Optimization refers to the process of finding the best-performing parameter for a system (for example, the number of days in a moving average) in historical testing and then assuming it will be the best parameter for trading in the future. This is rarely, if ever, the case. What you've done is simply found a parameter that best fits the precise behavior of past prices, which will never be repeated again. Optimization can be useful in finding a *range* of valid parameters. For example, you could test a moving average system and find that the best results are generated when the length of the moving average is between 40 and 50 days; you might then consider using the average length from this range as the parameter to trade in the future.

System fitting also can take the form of adding rule after rule to your trading system until it captures every quirk of the market during your test period—until it basically just *describes* past price action; it will almost certainly perform poorly in future trading. Strive for simplicity in your design. "Robust" systems that contain only a few parameters almost always outperform highly complex systems because the former are usually capturing universal market characteristics while the latter are merely curve-fit to the past. Also, by testing on multiple markets and longer time frames, you reduce the risk of creating an over-fit system.

HISTORICAL TESTING: GOALS AND LIMITATIONS

The goal of historical testing is to validate the profitability of an idea you have about the markets. But even after you find an idea that has proved to be profitable, you must be sure it makes money because it captures a logical, identifiable aspect of market behavior—not just because of a chance event. There has to be some sound logic underlying any system. To illustrate this point, we will use a simple trend-following system to guide us through the testing process. First, let's review the two main types of trading systems: trend-following and countertrend.

Trend-following systems measure the up or down movement in a market and establish a position in the direction of the current trend. The idea is that once a trend is established, the market will keep going in that direction until it reaches an equilibrium point, when prices will begin to go sideways and the position can be exited at a profit. While you may personally like or dislike this kind of trading approach, it's undeniably a rational description of market behavior and could make the basis for a profitable trading system. (That's what we'll find out in testing.)

Countertrend systems do just the opposite of trend-following systems. They determine the trend of a market and establish a position against it. The concept here is that markets are in equilibrium (that is, non-trending) most of the time and price moves are nothing more than short-term supply or demand imbalances that will quickly adjust themselves by prices moving in the opposite direction. Again, this is a logical argument upon which to consider basing a trading system.

Even though they are opposing approaches, both concepts are valid. Markets are in non-trending modes most of the time—about 80 percent of the time, in fact. On the other hand, markets also go through periods of price adjustment that create trends. But these periods are much less frequent because the fundamental facts of a market do not change from one day to the next. For example, when the U.S. economy goes into a recession, it can take several months or years to come out of it. During this time, the Federal Reserve Bank is usually in an interest rate-easing mode. It is no coincidence that the best trend-following techniques are usually longer-term systems. They tend to use more data to calculate buy and sell signals. This is not the case for countertrend techniques, most of which use less data to calculate buy and sell signals because they are not trying to measure the broader "fundamental picture." These systems are trying to exploit short-term supply and demand imbalances that have nothing to do with the overall fundamental state of a particular market.

A CASE STUDY

We are now ready to look at the testing results of actual trading systems—the channel breakout system, the moving average crossover system, and the moving average "fader" system—what they tell us about their advantages and disadvantages and how they might perform in real trading. Omega Research's TradeStation software was used to perform the historical testing, and Omega's Portfolio Maximizer to interpret the results. We tested the system on daily continuous T-bond futures from August 22, 1977, to August 28, 1998. (As noted, you should always test your system over multiple markets to get a more comprehensive perspective on its potential; we're just using the single market results to keep things simple.)

Many traders have used the channel breakout system with a good deal of success. The simplest kind of breakout system is sometimes referred to as a "stop-and-reverse" system. It goes long when price rises above the highest high of the last *n* days and goes short when price falls below the lowest low of the last *n* days. This system is always in the market: For example, a 40-day stop-and-reverse breakout system would buy on a new 40-day high and would hold that position until the market made a new 40-day low, at which point it would simultaneously liquidate the long position and establish a new short position (if you were long one contract, you would sell two contracts when the system reversed itself).

The basic breakout system can be modified several ways. One option is to use different channel lengths to enter and exit the market, which means the system will not always be in the market. Table 7.1 shows the results of using this kind of system with a 40-day price high for establishing long po-

TABLE 7.1
Channel Breakout System—System Analysis

Net Profit	$101,516.00	Open Position	($259.50)
Gross Profit	$369,689.25	Interest Earned	$52,309.15
Gross Loss	($268,173.25)	Commission Paid	$3,528.00
Percent Profitable	36.89%	Profit Factor	1.38
Ratio Avg. Win/Avg. Loss	2.36	Adjusted Profit Factor	1.05
Annual Rate of Return	3.50%	Sharpe Ratio	−0.09
Return on Initial Capital	101.52%	Return Retracement Ratio	0.25
Return on Max. Drawdown	1624.26%	K-Ratio	0.65
Buy/Hold Return	21.84%	RINA Index	41.48
Cumulative Return	33.50%	Percent in the Market	66.98%
Adjusted Net Profit	$15,844.80	Select Net Profit	$77,400.50
Adjusted Gross Profit	$314,579.23	Select Gross Profit	$345,573.75
Adjusted Gross Loss	($298,734.43)	Select Gross Loss	($268,173.25)

Source: Omega Research, Inc.

TABLE 7.2

Channel Breakout System—Time Analysis (Days)

Trading Period			
Years	20.62		
Months	247.40		
Weeks	1,072.05		
Days	7,525.00		
Time in the Market	5,094.00		
Percent in the Market	66.98%		
Longest Flat Period	64.00		
Avg. Time in Trades	40.95		
Avg. Time between Trades	20.15		
Avg. Time in Winning Trades	81.11		
Avg. Time between Winning Trades	84.86		
Avg. Time in Losing Trades	17.48		
Avg. Time between Losing Trades	80.11		
EQUITY CURVE ANALYSIS			
Avg. Time between peaks (days)	957.71	Notice length of time	
Maximum Equity Run-Up (daily)	$129,752.50	6/13/96	60.48%
Maximum Equity Drawdown (daily)	($56,590.00)	8/13/82	39.62%

Source: Omega Research, Inc.

sitions and a 20-day price low for getting out of those long positions (vice-versa for short trades).

The table shows the system has been profitable over the years. But what it doesn't show are the incredibly long time periods between new equity highs. Table 7.2 shows that the average number of days between new equity highs was

TABLE 7.3

Channel Breakout System—Annual Trading Summary

Annual Analysis (Mark-to-Market):

Period	Net Profit	% Gain	Profit Factor	# Trades	% Profitable
YTD	($2,307.50)	(1.12%)	0.00	3	0.00%
12 month	$173.50	0.09%	1.01	6	33.33%
97	$4,781.75	2.38%	1.62	6	50.00%
96	$4,683.00	2.39%	1.40	5	40.00%
95	$26,808.00	15.81%	4.85	5	60.00%
94	$8,385.00	5.20%	1.70	6	33.33%
93	$22,416.25	16.16%	4.41	5	60.00%
92	($17,542.50)	(11.22%)	0.29	9	33.33%
91	$5,897.25	3.92%	1.47	7	42.86%
90	$18,250.50	13.81%	3.30	5	60.00%
89	($4,386.25)	(3.21%)	0.77	7	28.57%
88	($4,235.00)	(3.01%)	0.69	7	42.86%
87	$11,156.75	8.61%	1.76	7	28.57%
86	($14,867.25)	(10.29%)	0.59	9	11.11%
85	$12,786.75	9.71%	1.81	7	42.86%
84	$32,337.00	32.55%	9.07	4	75.00%
83	($4,720.50)	(4.54%)	0.70	6	16.67%
82	($4,088.25)	(3.78%)	0.84	8	12.50%
81	($13,725.50)	(11.26%)	0.17	7	42.86%
80	$10,611.00	9.54%	1.68	7	57.14%
79	$5,467.00	5.17%	1.29	7	14.29%
78	$3,974.25	3.90%	1.47	7	42.86%
77	$1,824.75	1.82%	2.04	2	50.00%

Source: Omega Research, Inc.

957, and Table 7.3, the Annual Trading Summary, shows the system had eight losing years. This means the system made money in very short periods of time but then lan-

TABLE 7.4

Moving Average Crossover System—System Analysis

Net Profit	$49,156.25	Open Position	$3,000.00
Gross Profit	$236,375.00	Interest Earned	$0.00
Gross Loss	($187,218.75)	Commission Paid	$0.00
Percent Profitable	32.76%	Profit Factor	1.26
Ratio Avg. Win/Avg. Loss	2.59	Adjusted Profit Factor	1.00
Annual Rate of Return	1.19%	Sharpe Ratio	−0.28
Return on Initial Capital	27.89%	Return Retracement Ratio	0.22
Return on Max. Drawdown	914.53%	K-Ratio	−0.17
Buy/Hold Return	24.36%	RINA Index	6.17
Cumulative Return	51.26%	Percent in the Market	98.81%
Adjusted Net Profit	$539.24	Select Net Profit	$9,656.25
Adjusted Gross Profit	$205,066.37	Select Gross Profit	$196,875.00
Adjusted Gross Loss	($204,527.13)	Select Gross Loss	($107,218.75)

Source: Omega Research, Inc.

guished for much longer periods of time. It is quite obvious this system requires extreme patience; if you cannot wait two or three years between new equity highs, you run the risk of not letting the probabilities of the system play out (and as a result, quitting in frustration during a drawdown).

Next, we examine another trend-following approach, a traditional moving average crossover system, which goes long on the open the day after the 10-day moving average crosses above a 50-day moving average and goes short when the 10-day average crosses below the 50-day average. Table 7.4 shows that this system, like the channel breakout,

TABLE 7.5

Moving Average Crossover System—Time Analysis (Days)

Trading Period			
Years	20.72		
Months	248.61		
Weeks	1,077.33		
Days	7,562.00		
Time in the Market	7,585.00		
Percent in the Market	98.81%		
Longest Flat Period	0.00		
Avg. Time in Trades	43.46		
Avg. Time between Trades	0.00		
Avg. Time in Winning Trades	87.60		
Avg. Time between Winning Trades	45.34		
Avg. Time in losing Trades	21.96		
Avg. Time between Losing Trades	43.04		
Equity Curve Analysis			
Avg. Time between Peaks (days)	603.55		
Maximum Equity Run-Up (daily)	$65,187.50	5/8/96	27.23%
Maximum Equity Drawdown (daily)	($28,812.50)	7/14/82	14.05%

Source: Omega Research, Inc.

has been profitable over the years, and it also had long periods of negative performance. Examining Table 7.5, you can see that the average number of days between new equity highs was 603. Table 7.6, the Annual Trading Summary, shows the system had six losing years. This also

TABLE 7.6

Moving Average Crossover System—Annual Trading Summary

Annual Analysis (Mark-To-Market):

Period	Net Profit	% Gain	Profit Factor	# Trades	% Profitable
YTD	($9,812.50)	(4.17%)	0.23	13	15.38%
12 month	($4,625.00)	(2.01%)	0.68	13	23.08%
97	$3,093.75	1.33%	1.58	6	66.67%
96	$343.75	0.15%	1.03	12	25.00%
95	$19,437.50	0.15%	14.52	3	66.67%
94	$343.75	0.16%	1.03	12	25.00%
93	$8,718.75	4.29%	2.28	6	50.00%
92	($9,218.75)	(4.34%)	0.41	13	30.77%
91	$781.25	0.37%	1.08	11	36.36%
90	$3,562.50	1.71%	1.44	8	50.00%
89	($468.75)	(0.22%)	0.94	10	20.00%
88	$4,093.75	2.00%	1.67	11	27.27%
87	($1,531.25)	(0.74%)	0.87	9	33.33%
86	$3,906.25	1.93%	1.27	9	33.33%
85	$7,656.25	3.94%	1.82	9	33.33%
84	$12,531.25	6.89%	3.55	6	33.33%
83	($6,093.75)	(3.24%)	0.44	10	30.00%
82	$5,218.75	2.85%	1.74	8	12.50%
81	($12,406.25)	(6.35%)	0.32	12	33.33%
80	$9,312.50	5.01%	1.58	9	33.33%
79	$3,406.25	1.87%	1.59	10	20.00%
78	$5,187.50	2.93%	3.59	7	57.14%
77	$1,093.75	0.62%	2.94	2	50.00%

Source: Omega Research, Inc.

means the system makes money in very short periods of time but languishes for much longer periods of time.

The long periods of flat- to down-equity these systems exhibit is typical of long-term trend-following techniques. If we examine Tables 7.3 and 7.6, we notice the high correlation of losing years on both systems. This is not coincidental since both systems are based on price momentum continuing in one direction. There are just not enough major fundamental changes in the U.S. bond market to support sustained price moves in either direction.

Improving system performance

What can we do to improve our system trading performance? One option is to diversify our systems to alleviate the negative qualities described in the previous section.

Let's look at a countertrend technique and see how it affects the equity curve. I'll use the "moving average fader" system, which is when a short-term strategy takes the opposite positions of a traditional moving average crossover system. It uses a 3-day moving average and a 10-day moving average. However, when the 3-day average goes below the 10-day average, we buy the next day on the open. Normally, a trend-following system in this situation would trade in the direction of the price momentum and go short. To exit a position, we wait for one day to pass and exit the next day at the close (vice versa for shorts).

As you can see by Table 7.7, the system made money over the test period. Like the Channel Breakout System, it has long periods of negative performance. Examining Table 7.8 reveals that the average number of days between new equity highs was 219, significantly lower than either of our

TABLE 7.7

Moving Average "Fader" System—System Analysis

Net Profit	$53,781.25	Open Position	($2,531.25)
Gross Profit	$612,375.00	Interest Earned	$46,774.74
Gross Loss	($558,593.75)	Commission Paid	$0.00
Percent Profitable	66.46%	Profit Factor	1.10
Ratio Avg. Win/Avg. Loss	0.55	Adjusted Profit Factor	1.03
Annual Rate of Return	1.29%	Sharpe Ratio	−0.09
Return on Initial Capital	30.51%	Return Retracement Ratio	0.14
Return on Max. Drawdown	685.66%	K-Ratio	1.79
Buy/Hold Return	25.59%	RINA Index	232.42
Cumulative Return	50.87%	Percent in the Market	76.37%
Adjusted Net Profit	$15,252.06	Select Net Profit	$118,812.50
Adjusted Gross Profit	$606,607.15	Select Gross Profit	$579,062.50
Adjusted Gross Loss	($580,255.09)	Select Gross Loss	($460,250.00)

Source: Omega Research, Inc.

trend-following systems. Table 7.9, the Annual Trading Summary for this system, shows the system suffered eight losing years. However, the important feature of this system is the non-correlation of its losing years to those of the trend-following systems: Only one (1981) coincided with the losing years trend-following systems. This means that if we traded the countertrend system along with the trend-following systems, we are no longer in a position of possibly waiting years to make new equity highs in our account.

TABLE 7.8
Moving Average "Fader" System—Time Analysis (Days)

Trading Period			
Years	20.81		
Months	249.70		
Weeks	1,082.03		
Days	7,595.00		
Time in the Market	5,862.00		
Percent in the Market	76.37%		
Longest Flat Period	5.00		
Avg. Time in Trades	2.95		
Avg. Time between Trades	0.88		
Avg. Time in Winning Trades	2.03		
Avg. Time between Winning Trades	3.74		
Avg. Time in Losing Trades	4.78		
Avg. Time between Losing Trades	6.61		
EQUITY CURVE ANALYSIS			
Avg. Time between Peaks (days)	(219.38)	MUCH LESS THAN 957	
Maximum Equity Run-Up (daily)	$92,031.25	4/13/98	39.68%
Maximum Equity Drawdown (daily)	($40,250.00)	4/1/86	22.30%

Source: Omega Research, Inc.

Table 7.10, which is a combined equity table for the combined channel breakout system and the moving average fader system, illustrates the benefits of combining systems: There were only four losing years, significantly fewer than the trend-following system by itself. In addition to the obvi-

TABLE 7.9

Moving Average "Fader" System—Annual Trading Summary

Annual Analysis (Mark-To-Market):

Period	Net Profit	% Gain	Profit Factor	# Trades	% Profitable
YTD	$7,593.75	3.41%	1.72	60	60.00%
12 month	$15,937.50	7.44%	2.25	82	59.76%
97	$17,562.50	8.57%	2.19	88	56.82%
96	$3,781.25	1.88%	1.15	87	51.72%
95	($2,375.00)	(1.17%)	0.92	91	48.35%
94	$13,781.25	7.26%	1.72	94	52.13%
93	$9,312.50	5.16%	1.41	87	51.72%
92	$562.50	0.31%	1.03	88	46.59%
91	$11,375.00	6.75%	1.56	97	49.48%
90	$8,281.25	5.17%	1.33	92	53.26%
89	$5,031.25	3.24%	1.28	92	55.43%
88	$6,312.50	4.24%	1.25	90	47.92%
87	($7,718.75)	(4.93%)	0.80	99	38.38%
86	$7,031.25	4.70%	1.16	114	34.21%
85	($10,437.50)	(6.52%)	0.68	105	35.24%
84	($6,437.50)	(3.87%)	0.75	105	37.14%
83	$3,656.25	2.25%	1.17	90	41.11%
82	$6,562.50	4.20%	1.22	105	50.48%
81	($11,031.25)	(6.60%)	0.73	96	37.50%
80	($8,843.75)	(5.02%)	0.85	102	37.25%
79	($62.50)	(0.04%)	1.00	102	40.20%
78	$1,343.75	0.77%	1.10	96	47.92%
77	($1,437.50)	(0.82%)	0.45	12	41.67%

Source: Omega Research, Inc.

ous monetary benefits, this diversification makes it psychologically easier to maintain trading discipline over long periods of time, enhancing your odds of ultimate success.

TABLE 7.10

Combined equity for channel breakout system and moving average fader system (both systems trading same number of contracts)

Date	Equity	Net Profit
Dec. 78	531	531
Dec. 79	531	0
Dec. 80	12,093	11,562
Dec. 81	14,125	2,032
Dec. 82	−10,343	−24,468
Dec. 83	−7,437	2,906
Dec. 84	−8,093	−656
Dec. 85	18,093	26,186
Dec. 86	20,875	2,782
Dec. 87	13,375	−7,500
Dec. 88	17,125	3,750
Dec. 89	19,562	2,437
Dec. 90	20,687	1,125
Dec. 91	47,531	26,844
Dec. 92	65,187	17,656
Dec. 93	48,687	−16,500
Dec. 94	80,656	31,969
Dec. 95	103,062	22,406
Dec. 96	127,687	24,625
Dec. 97	136,343	8,656
Dec. 98	159,000	22,657

Source: Omega Research, Inc.

It's easier to follow systems when you have a sense you're making money throughout most of your trading campaign.

LEVERAGE

Leverage, which is the amount of capital allocated to a particular trade, is one of the most important concepts for any trader to understand. During my career, I've seen many traders with sound trading plans get wiped out because of one simple fact: over-leveraging.

How do you determine how much equity to commit to a trade? The first thing we examine is the largest equity drawdown for each system. This is the largest peak-to-valley dip that a hypothetical account would have gone through had it been trading this system in the past. Now we must ask ourselves the probability that this will repeat itself in the future. From my experience, the largest drawdown in the past will not only be repeated in the future, it will probably be exceeded. Why? Because as you add more data to your test, you almost always get the same result: larger drawdowns. As a result, we must also use other more commonsense measures to determine the amount of leverage to use.

I always look at what I call the "leverage ratio," which is simply the dollar amount of your positions divided by the account equity. For example, if we were trading U.S. Treasury bonds, one contract at a price of 125 is equal to $125,000 (125 × $1,000 per point). If we had $50,000 in our account, then our leverage ratio would be 2.5 ($125,000/$50,000). For every dollar we have, we are controlling 2.5

dollars. I recommend keeping your leverage ratio at 6 or lower.

CONCLUSION

System trading offers certain advantages that appeal to many traders: If forces discipline on traders who may need it and removes emotion from the trading process. Historical testing can benefit even discretionary traders because system test results can give a trader a better understanding of a basic trading approach—its strengths and flaws—and how it might behave in the future.

It's important to take steps to keep you system tests realistic and honest, though. Factor in accurate commissions and slippage and don't over-optimize your systems—simpler approaches tend to work better than complex ones. Use trading ideas that capture logical, inherent market characteristics, and test your system over many markets and a long enough time frame to give you a realistic picture of its potential.

Our specific tests results revealed some weaknesses in a couple of popular trading approaches, but also showed how diversifying between systems whose drawdowns occur at different times can improve your overall trading performance. Finally, remember that over-leveraging can blow you and your system out of the water. Proper risk control and money management are just as important in system trading as they are in any other kind of trading. Strict risk control rules should be an integral part of any trading system.

Risk Control: The Foundation of My Trading Success

by Mark Boucher

Mark Boucher, professional hedge fund manager and trader, has been the manager of the Midas Trust Fund, Cayman Islands, since 1992. In 1998, the fund was ranked number one in the world by Nelson's World's Best Money Managers for its five-year annual compounded rate of return of 26.6 percent. He also is the author of the highly-acclaimed book The Hedge Fund Edge: Maximum Profit/Minimum Risk Global Trend Trading Strategies *(1999, John Wiley & Sons).*

Mr. Boucher began trading at age 16. His profits helped finance his education at the University of California at Berkeley, from which he graduated with honors in Economics. Upon graduation, he founded Investment Research Associates to finance research on stock, bond, and currency trading systems. Mr. Boucher joined forces with Fortunet, Inc., in 1986, where he developed models for hedging and trading bonds, currencies, futures, and stocks. In 1989, the results of his research were published in the Fortunet Trading Course. While with Fortunet, Mr. Boucher also applied this research to designing institutional products, such as a hedging model on over $1 billion of debt exposure for the treasurer of Mead, a Fortune 500 company. The material in this chapter is adapted from The Hedge Fund Edge *with permission from John Wiley & Sons Publishers, New York.*

Strategy and money management are the two most important parts of my, and any successful trader's, overall plan—the foundation upon which all trading success is built. Winning traders know that the best entry rule in the world is useless without proper risk control. You can almost perfectly analyze a developing market situation, find the best strategy to exploit that situation, and be almost perfectly correct in your forecast of what that market will do, and yet you can still lose money if you do not use proper risk control and money management. As successful futures trader Stanley Kroll once noted, "It is better to have a mediocre system and good money management than an excellent system and poor money management."

While top traders understand that money management is the most critical element of long-run investment success, it is unfortunately the area where most up-and-coming traders and investors make the most mistakes. Summarized below are what I consider to be some of the most important money management rules I've developed and learned in my years as a professional trader. I suggest you go over these rules before entering any trade, and that you review them after completing each trade to make sure you adhere to them.

HIGH-PERFORMANCE MONEY MANAGEMENT RULES

1. *Always use protective stops when you enter a new position to limit your theoretical risk on each trade.* Theoretical risk is the distance between your entry price and your "open protective stop" (OPS). If you buy a stock at 10 and place an OPS at 8, your theoretical risk is 2 points (10 – 8 = 2). If you want to keep drawdowns less than 25 percent (a good idea), you should limit your theoretical risk on each position to 2 percent or less of capital. In other words, if you have a $100,000 account you should only risk $2000 per trade in theoretical risk. If you buy a stock at 10 with an OPS at 8, you can buy no more than 1000 shares because 1000 shares times 2 points equals a theoretical risk of $2000. If you purchase more than 1000 shares, you would be taking excessive theoretical risk.

2. *Use trailing stops to lock in profits as a trade moves in your favor.* For example, when the market moves significantly in your favor on a long position, then consolidates or retraces, and then posts a new high, move your OPS up to below the last strong support level to protect profits as the market

FIGURE 8.1

FIGURE 8.1

Trailing Stops: Dell Computer (DELL), Daily

Dell Computer Corp-Daily 01/26/99 C=84.875 +1.875 O=83.625 H=85.000 L=81.250

Progressively tighter trailing stops used to protect profits in up trend (placed at bottom of corrections)

Source: Omega Research, Inc.

moves up (just as you protected initial risk when you first entered the trade). When using trailing stops, make sure to always let the market's own price action determine where OPSs or trailing stops are placed. Figure 8.1 shows an example of how trailing stops could be placed at the support levels offered by retracements throughout the course of a long up trend.

3. *Use "Creeping Commitment" to start with a small position and build to a larger one as your trailing stop eliminates your risk to initial capital.* Suppose we bought a stock at 10 with an OPS at 8. The stock then moves up to 15, where it con-

solidates for many weeks between 13 and 15 before breaking out to new highs again. As long as the stock is not overvalued or over-owned you can add to the position as long as your new OPS is above the entry price of the last position (so there is no theoretical risk on the prior position). Your commitment to a stock or commodity can creep higher only in those trades that show strong profits and continue to meet this criteria.

4. *Allocation rule: Never invest more than 25 percent of your portfolio capital in any one stock or market sector, and begin divesting when an issue or sector grows beyond 33 percent of your portfolio.*

5. *For longer-term multimarket traders: Diversify among two to six instruments in any one sector; don't "de-worsify" among more than 10 unless market risk and uncertainly are unusually high.* You get most of the benefits of diversification with a portfolio of 6 to 10 stocks, for example.

6. *For longer-term trades, let your profits run on any position until it is either overvalued, over-owned, or stopped out via trailing stops.* Often, a trend will run far longer than you might initially suspect. Let your goal be to stay invested in strong trends for as long as they run, as long as chronic overvaluation or over-ownership does not exist.

7. *Never average a loss.* This is a recipe for disaster. I never add to a position until I show a net profit on prior positions. You want to build positions in markets that are moving powerfully in your direction, not against you.

8. *Limit your total portfolio risk to 20 percent.* If you were stopped out of every one of your open trades, your losses should not exceed 20 percent of your portfolio. Always ask yourself, if there were some catastrophe and I was stopped out of absolutely every position in my portfolio, what would my total risk be? Even in the most stable environment, keep this number at 20 percent, and lower it to 15 percent or less during uncertain times. This will help keep your maximum drawdowns to less-than-disastrous levels and keep you in the game for the long haul.

GENERAL RULES

9. *When in doubt, stay out or get out—and don't get back in until you are sure about a position.* I enter a position only when several methods indicate the trade is reliable and has strong profit potential in relation to risk. There is nothing wrong with sitting heavily in cash or bonds while waiting for the right combination of reliability, risk/reward, and technical signals to show up.

10. *Concentrate most of your time and effort on selecting the best markets to trade.* Focus on finding reliable trends in top markets where low-risk, high-quality trades are developing. Many traders spend more than half their time on arcane theories designed to help them pinpoint exact high and low points for the overall market. Unfortunately, they are putting too much of their valuable time on an area that actually has much less impact on their profitability than market selection. You want to spend most of your time and effort

on the areas that have the greatest effect on your performance, and that means market selection.

11. *Remember that markets are an odds game—they are not predictable.* The most brilliant trader or analyst on earth is in trouble if he is heavily long Semiconductor stocks and Korean manufacturers flood the market with a new, low-priced computer chip. Many events that affect the markets are not predictable, while even those events that appear predictable do not have the expected effect every time. Strive to follow the markets and let them confirm your analysis before investing heavily, and be sure to use the risk containment rules outlined earlier just in case you get hit by an unforeseen, market-jolting event. Also, prepare to be wrong periodically, even when you are very sure about a particular trend continuing. Being wrong is part of the business; take your lumps and move on. Even the best quarterback throws an occasional interception—that's part of the game. You must learn to accept losses and not let mistakes detour you from your goals and strategy.

12. *Only recapitalize your profits when you have earned more than enough to cover your expected maximum drawdown.* Recapitalization is the process of using profits to resize your portfolio risk parameters. If you start the year with $100,000 and build 35 percent profits by year-end, the next year you can base your risk rules on a $135,000 portfolio starting point only when your maximum drawdown is expected to be less than 35 percent. A good rule of thumb for maximum drawdown estimates is 1.5 times your maximum

portfolio risk. Thus, if you follow my 20 percent maximum portfolio risk rule, you should only recapitalize once you have achieved a 30 percent or greater profit.

13. *Keep a trading journal and review and evaluate your trades and decisions periodically.* This may be the most important rule for most traders. A trading journal should have a "before picture" and an "after picture" of every trade you make. When you make a trade, print out a chart of it with an arrow where you bought or sold along with every reason you had for putting on the position, including where your initial OPS is and your plan for exiting the position. Every time you change stops or adjust the position, print out another chart, showing where and explaining why. When you exit (partially or totally), print out another chart and give your reasons. Did you follow the initial plan you outlined on your entry chart printout? Why or why not? What did you learn about the markets? What did you learn about yourself? What rules might help you to avoid any problems that developed?

This is the type of painstaking analysis a trader must make on each and every trade. Then, every 30 trades or so (or every quarter or at least twice a year), you should review this journal and the decisions of the latest period. Make sure you are following your trading plan and note periodic mistakes and bad habits. Then make a plan for compensating for and correcting these errors and weaknesses. I've noticed that traders have a tendency to look for new strategies outside of themselves when they have poorer-than-desired performance. Don't fall into this trap. More often than not, the problem is not with your strategy, but with your execution of it; the problem is internal, not external. If this is the case, a new strategy will not solve the problem; it will merely allow you to shift the blame.

A good trading journal is the tool of almost every great trader I have ever studied or heard of. It gives you the means to correct internal problems and to evaluate and get feedback on what you're doing. Few traders and investors who have religiously kept a journal for more than a few years remain market losers.

14. *Markets normally move in trends with three to five sections or legs.* Even if you are a very short-term trader, it pays to be aware of the market context in which you are operating. Try to know the secular trend (i.e., many years over many liquidity cycles), cyclical trend (usually three to six years in a liquidity cycle of recession to expansion), intermediate-trend (many months), and short-term trend (days to weeks) in any market or sector you are contemplating trading in.

15. *Buy strength and sell weakness.* Let your goal be to find exceptional strength where there is still room on the upside or to find exceptional weakness where there is still room on the downside. Remember, positioning yourself in strong trends allows you to improve the reliability of your trading, but it does not limit the upside potential. In fact, catching a reaction or breakout in a strong trend is usually far more profitable on a risk/reward basis than catching the bottom or top of a market.

16. *Let your profits run and cut your losses short with OPSs and trailing stops.*

17. *Remember that price makes news; news does not make price.* Markets are discounting mechanisms and leading indicators. As such, they strive to anticipate the next six to twelve months of economically relevant action. News is only important in how it changes expectations of the future outlook.

18. *Watch closely how a market reacts to news that should be construed as clearly positive or clearly negative.* When a market reacts negatively to clearly positive news, it is telling you the news is less important than prices have already expected and the market is particularly vulnerable. In this situation, you should immediately lighten up on your long positions. Similarly, when a market reacts positively to clearly bearish news, it is particularly susceptible to short-covering or accumulation, and you should cut back on shorts. A strange reaction to news tells you what expectations have already been built into price. It is a warning sign prudent investors should heed.

CONCLUSION

I've seen more than a few traders pay lip service to risk management while trying feverishly to find "holy grail" entry and exit rules. Placing more importance on trade signals than on risk control and money management is putting the cart before the horse. The best trade signals in the

FIGURE 8.2

A Few Money Management Benchmarks

Risk Area	Benchmark
Per-trade risk	Limit to 2 percent (or less) of trading capital
Total portfolio risk	Limit to 20 percent of trading capital (15 percent in uncertain periods)
Exposure to a particular stock or sector	No more than 25 percent of capital; divest when above 33 percent
Drawdowns	25 percent maximum

world will only lose you money if they are not accompanied by risk control rules that limit your exposure and money management rules that maximize your profit potential. Figure 8.2 summarizes some of the risk benchmarks we discussed in this chapter. For long-term success, find the best markets to trade, apply these trading and risk control rules conscientiously, and keep a trading journal to monitor your progress.

CHAPTER 9

Additional Trading Strategies and Concepts

Here are several additional trading methods used by the cofounders of TRADEHARD.COM. Like those from the previous chapters, these diverse and innovative approaches share common strengths: They use specific price patterns that exploit inherent market conditions, which, when combined with strict risk control, keep the odds in your favor over the long haul.

HOT IPO PULLBACKS

High-publicity initial public offerings (IPOs) offer some of the best profit opportunities for heads-up stock traders. But because institutions receive the lion's share of most hot IPOs, it's next to impossible to get shares in good companies when they go public. That doesn't have to be the end of the story, though. We have found that the next best way to get on board these dynamic stocks is to buy them after they have pulled back and then resumed their up trends.

The approach is simple:

1. Identify a company that has traded at least 15 percent higher within five trading days after going public. This means if the deal is priced at 20, the stock must trade higher than 23 in its first five days of trading.

2. Wait for a two- to four-day pullback, which can take any number of price bar combinations—lower lows, lower closes, inside days, and so on (the examples will clarify this).

3. After the second, third, or fourth day of the pullback, buy 1/16 point above the previous day's high.

4. Place your initial protective stop at the previous day's low.

5. Hold the position from one to five days, using trailing stops to protect profits.

The trades shown in Figures 9.1 and 9.2 give an idea of how well this strategy can work. In Figure 9.1, International

FIGURE 9.1

Hot IPO Pullback: International Network Services (INSS), Daily

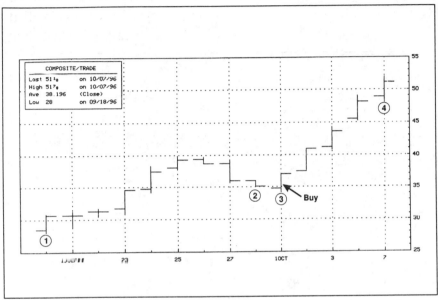

Source: Bloomberg LP.

Network Services (INSS) goes public at $16 and opens at $28 1/2 (1)—well over 15 percent above the offering price, qualifying it as a "hot" stock. After a three-day pullback (2), we buy 1/16 above the high of September 30, getting filled at 36 1/16 on October 1 (3). We place our stop near the September 30 low of 35. The market takes off and within a week we're sitting on an approximately 40 percent profit (4).

Figure 9.2 tells a similar story in Advanced Fiber Communications (AFCI). On October 1, the stock goes public at 25 and opens at 38 3/4 (1), again, above our 15 percent threshold. After a three-day pullback (2), we get filled at 50 1/16 when the trend resumes (3). Our initial stop is near the pre-

FIGURE 9.2

Hot IPO Pullback: Advanced Fiber Communications (AFCI), Daily

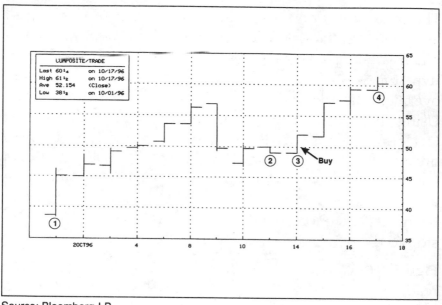

Source: Bloomberg LP.

vious day's low of 49. The market rallies 10 points over the next three days (4).

2-FOR-1 MONEY MANAGEMENT

The question of where to take profits is a never-ending dilemma for all professional traders. Choosing between locking in gains and letting profits run can be a gut-wrenching experience. Many top traders have found that using an approach like the "2-for-1" money management method helps alleviate this dilemma by reconciling these two trading objectives. It improves any trading method by automatically keeping probabilities on your side.

The concept is simple: liquidate *half* a position at a reward level equal to the risk level for the total position. For example, if you buy 1000 shares of a stock at 60 and your protective stop is at 58, you are risking two points (barring an overnight disaster and ignoring slippage and commissions). Using the 2-for-1 method, you would sell 500 shares at 62 (1:1 risk/reward). You would then move your stop to breakeven (60) on the remaining 500 shares. The worse-case scenario is that you break even on second half of the trade and make two points on the first half. Depending on other factors impacting a particular trade, you can use a trailing stop to let the remaining 500 shares run.

Figure 9.3 shows this approach in action. A low volatility reading in the June 1998 Japanese yen (1) sets up a buy signal pending a reversal of the initial down move (2). A long position is triggered at 7592 when the yen gaps open (4). We place a protective stop below the prior day's low (3) at 7546, giving us a risk of 46 points. The market explodes higher, hitting our initial profit target of 7638 (our entry fill of 7592 plus 46 points). We immediately sell half the position and raise our stop on the remaining half to one point above our original entry point (7593).

The market opens below the protective stop (5) and we are stopped out for a loss of nine ticks on the second half of the position. As you can see, without profit taking and the trailing stop, this profitable position would have turned into a loser.

FIGURE 9.3

2-for-1 Money Management: Japanese Yen

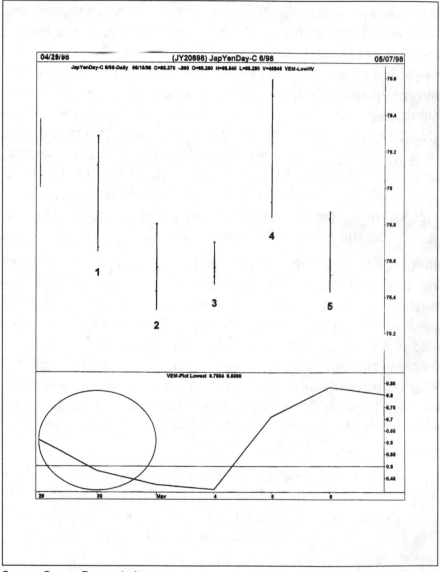

Source: Omega Research, Inc.

NEWS REVERSALS

We have all seen a company announce better-than-expected earnings before the opening, gap higher, and then collapse. The same kind of thing happens in futures markets upon the release of important government reports or economic news. How do you take advantage of these quick, extreme swings in market sentiment? With a strategy called News Reversals.

A setup occurs when a big news event is released after the market closes one day and causes the market to gap higher or lower the next day. For example, if a very bullish crop report was released on Monday after the close, excitement over the next day's trading builds to a fever pitch overnight, and on Tuesday morning a buying frenzy takes place on the opening. The market does gap higher—much higher—creating a short-term overbought condition. Instead of rallying further, the market begins to sag. Next, short sellers start pushing the market lower, forcing the nervous longs to abandon their positions; more sellers continue to enter the market, erasing the morning's gains. What was originally thought to be a long-term buying opportunity turns out to be a short-term selling opportunity for shrewd traders who see the potential of bucking the herd.

These are the rules:

1. Wait for an extremely bullish or bearish event to occur after the close. For stock traders, this could mean an earnings report, analyst recommendation, and so on. For futures traders, it could be an

economic report, crop or livestock report, weather report, and so on.

2. For a signal to occur, the day after the new release, the market must gap open above or below the previous day's high or low. (In some markets, news may be released the same day long enough before the opening that it has the same effect as an announcement the previous day. In these cases, the trade is obviously taken the same day as the announcement, not the following day.)

3. When the market gaps up, enter a sell stop one tick below the previous day's high. When the market gaps down, enter a buy stop one tick above the previous day's low.

4. Place a protective stop that risks no more than today's low or high (or less, if such a stop level represents excessive risk). When the market moves in your favor, use a trailing stop to lock in profits.

Let's take a look at some examples.

In Figure 9.4 a bullish cotton report is released before the opening bell on August 25, 1998. Cotton initially gaps open above the previous day's high and rallies slightly. We place a sell stop to enter the market one tick below the previous day's high. The market quickly reverses and we are filled on our order; we place a protective stop near today's high.

Cotton ends up closing much lower on the day, and four trading sessions later, it is trading nearly 5 cents below our entry level.

FIGURE 9.4

News Reversals: Cotton, Daily

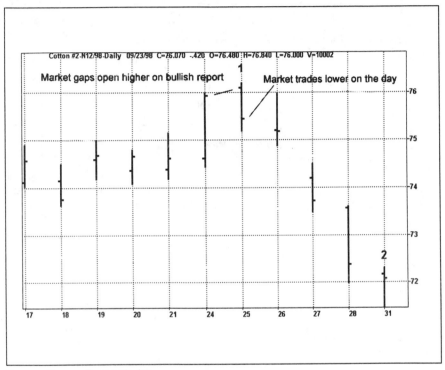

Source: Omega Research, Inc.

Figure 9.5 shows the results when a better-than-expected cattle report is released before the open. The market initially gaps higher on April 17, 1998, but quickly reverses. Again, we get short a tick below the previous day's high and place a protective stop just above today's high after we are filled. Within the next four trading sessions, cattle is more than $4 lower.

FIGURE 9.5
News Reversals: Live Cattle, Daily

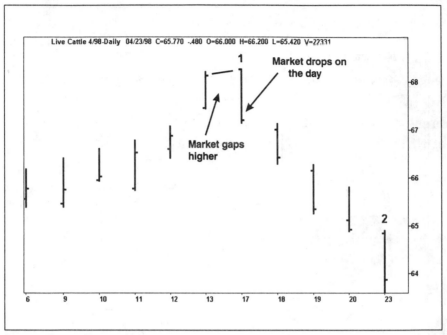

Source: Omega Research, Inc.

FUTURES TRADERS: 20-DAY HIGH/LOW POINTS ARE THE KEY

Futures that make new 20-day highs or new 20-day lows attract a lot of attention. The majority of commodity trading advisors (CTAs), for example, use these levels to enter breakout positions. As a direct result of this popularity, however, such simple breakout strategies have become less reliable over time—false signals are rampant, and the unwary trader can get whipsawed repeatedly before catching a good trade.

But there are ways to turn this state of affairs to your advantage. The Turtle Soup strategy, described in the book *Street Smarts* by Larry Connors and Linda Bradford Raschke, effectively turns the 20-day breakout on its head by taking signals in the *opposite* direction of the initial breakout—capitalizing on the more numerous false signals at these key 20-day high/low junctures.

These are the rules for buys; for sells, reverse:

1. **Day One:** The market must first make a new 20-day low, and the previous 20-day low must have occurred at least four days earlier. The close of the new low day must be the same or lower than the previous 20-day low.

2. **Day Two:** Enter the market on a buy stop order placed the next day at the previous 20-day low. *If the order is not filled on this day, cancel the trade.*

3. If the order is filled, place a protective sell stop-loss order (good-till-canceled) one tick under the lower of the lows of Day One or Day Two.

4. Take partial profits within two to six days and use a trailing stop on the rest of the position to guard profits.

These trades can last anywhere from a few hours to a few days. A few examples will help illustrate the strategy.

FIGURE 9.6

Turtle Soup: September 98 Copper, Daily

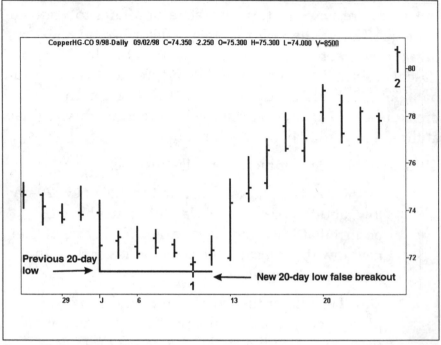

CopperHG-CO 9/98-Daily   09/02/98 C=74.350 -2.250 O=75.300 H=75.300 L=74.000 V=8500

Previous 20-day low →

New 20-day low false breakout ←

Source: Omega Research, Inc.

Figure 9.6 shows that on July 9, 1998, September copper futures made a new 20-day low, which turned out to be a false breakout followed by a powerful move in the opposite direction. The previous 20-day low was at least four trading sessions earlier, fulfilling the other entry requirement. We place a buy stop order just above the prior 20-day low at 71.60. After getting filled, we place a GTC sell stop one tick under the day's low. Copper subsequently traded over 9 cents higher. The initial stop would have been raised as the

FIGURE 9.7

Turtle Soup: September 98 Copper, Daily

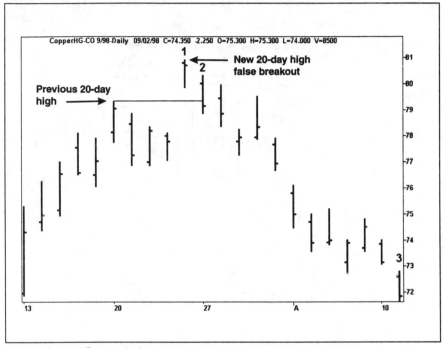

CopperHG-CO 9/98-Daily 09/02/98 C=74.350 -2.250 O=75.300 H=75.300 L=74.000 V=8500

New 20-day high false breakout

Previous 20-day high

Source: Omega Research, Inc.

market moved in the direction of the trade, trailing the position to protect profits.

Now look at figure 9.7. Later in the month on July 26, September copper futures made a new 20-day high. Again, the previous 20-day high occurred at least four trading sessions earlier, validating the potential entry signal. The next day, copper reversed and traded below the prior 20-day high. We go short on a stop order at 79.10, just below that high. Copper futures lost more than 7 cents over the next two weeks.

FIGURE 9.8

Turtle Soup: Amazon.com (AMZN), Daily

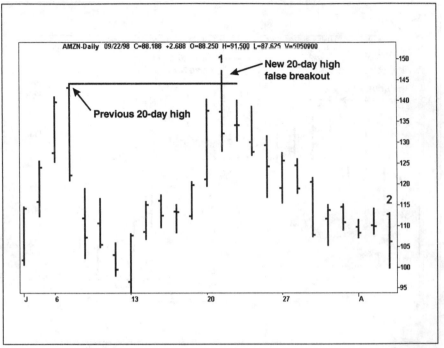

Source: Omega Research, Inc.

Figure 9.8 shows a Turtle Soup example in the stock market. On July 21, 1998, Amazon.com (AMZN) makes a 20-day high and reverses with the previous 20-day high at least four trading days earlier. We go short at 143.50, just below the prior 20-day high. AMZN drops 36 points over the next two weeks.

FIGURE 9.9

Turtle Soup: D-Mark, Daily

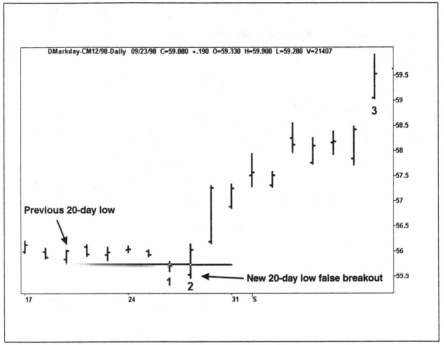

DMarkday-CM12/98-Daily 09/23/98 C=59.880 +.190 O=59.330 H=59.900 L=59.280 V=21407

Previous 20-day low

New 20-day low false breakout

Source: Omega Research, Inc.

In Figure 9.9, December D-mark futures make a new 20-day low on August 26, 1998, with the previous 20-day low having fallen at least four trading sessions earlier. The D-mark reverses up through the previous 20-day low, triggering a long position at 5583 (just above the low).

FIGURE 9.10

Turtle Soup: Johnson & Johnson (JNJ), Daily

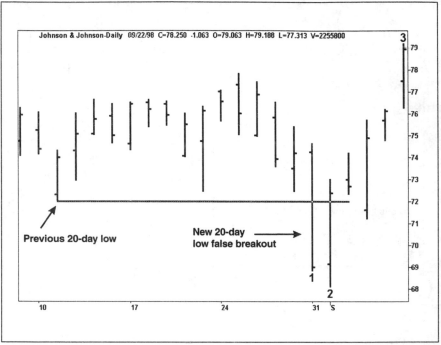

Source: Omega Research, Inc.

Figure 9.10 is our final Turtle Soup example. On August 31, 1998, Johnson & Johnson (JNJ) makes a new 20-day low. The previous 20-day low was at least four trading days earlier. The next day, JNJ trades above the prior 20-day low, triggering a long trade at 72 3/8, just above that low. The result: JNJ rallies more than 6 1/2 points over the next four days.

CONNORS VIX REVERSAL I (CVR I)

The VIX is a volatility index calculated by the Chicago Board Options Exchange (CBOE). High VIX readings typically signify highly volatile markets that are declining, and low VIX reads usually reflect quiet rising markets. The CVR I is a method developed by Larry Connors that uses the VIX to identify likely market reversal points. These are the rules for buy orders:

1. Today the VIX must make a 15-day high.

2. Today the close of the VIX must be below the open.

3. If Rule 1 is met, buy on today's close (you will have to watch the market and make this decision in the last few minutes of trading).

4. Hold the position at least one to three days.

Here are the rules for sell orders:

1. Today the VIX must make a 15-day low.

2. Today the close of the VIX must be above the open.

3. If Rule 1 is met, sell on today's close (you will have to watch the market and make this decision in the last few minutes of trading).

4. Hold the position at least one to three days.

FIGURE 9.11
CVRI: S&P 500 and VIX

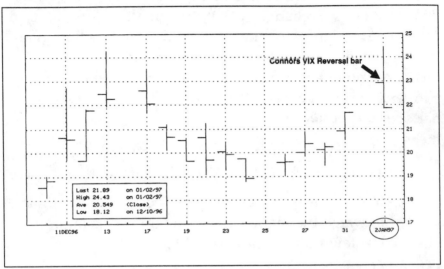

Source: Bloomberg LP.

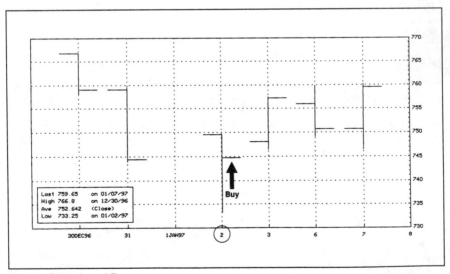

Source: Bloomberg LP.

Figure 9.11 shows what a CVR I signal looks like. Notice the buy signal triggered in the S&P 500 futures on January 2, 1998, which corresponds to the CVR reversal bar on the same date. The market moved up 25 points over the next three days.

From 1990 to 1999, this signal has correctly identified approximately two-thirds of seven-day market tops and bottoms. The technique works because the VIX essentially measures trader behavior. During sell-offs, traders panic and rush to buy puts, driving up their value. When this panic ceases to persist intraday, the market reverses, driving prices higher. This is why the VIX closes below where it opens at these times.

WHEN STOCKS DO WHAT THEY SHOULDN'T

This is a cousin of the News Reversals strategy described earlier in the chapter. Each day, look for stocks that moved in the opposite direction of a major brokerage house change. A stock that rises in the face of negative news is, in effect, shouting out an old Wall Street adage: "If it doesn't go down on bad news, it's going higher." A stock that declines in the face of positive news is shouting the opposite. Figure 9.12 provides an excellent example.

FIGURE 9.12

When Stocks Do What They Shouldn't:
Wal-Mart (WMT), Daily

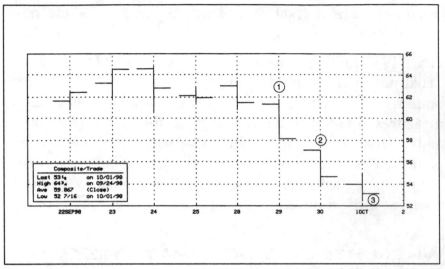

Source: Bloomberg LP.

1. B.T. Alex Brown bumps up their opinion of
   Wal-Mart to a "strong buy."

2. Because the stock declined yesterday on positive
   news, we go short at 57 (the opening) and risk 1
   point placing a protective stop at 58.

3. Wal-Mart plunges more than four points (intraday)
   from our entry point.

FIGURE 9.13

When Stocks Do What They Shouldn't:
Dow Chemical (DOW), Daily

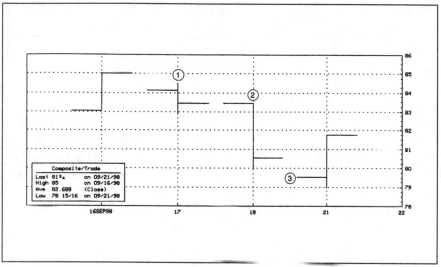

Source: Bloomberg LP.

Figure 9.13, Dow Chemical, tells a similar story. Merrill Lynch puts out a buy recommendation on Dow, but the stock still drops (1). We sell short at 82 13/16 (2), and Dow gaps open lower at 79 1/2 the next day.

FIGURE 9.14
Down Trending Markets with Late Earnings:
Baby Superstores, Daily

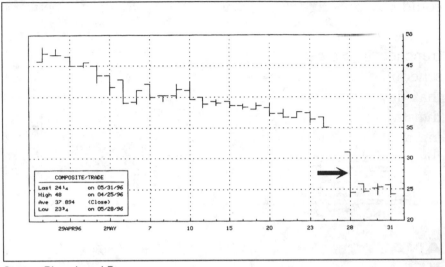

Source: Bloomberg LP.

SHORT SELLERS: JUMP ON DOWN-TRENDING STOCKS WITH LATE EARNINGS REPORTS

Stocks often sag before announcing bad earnings, primarily because word leaks out and the "smart money" bails out of their positions. When they also announce their earnings late, it is usually a signal that the bad news has taken management by surprise and they are in damage control mode—trying to cook up a "strategic plan" to announce to Wall Street. The rule of thumb in these situations is "look out below!" These are often excellent short selling opportunities.

A stock both trading under its 20-day moving average and late in announcing earnings is an excellent candidate to short. As an alternative to an outright short position, you could buy puts to define your risk on the trade.

Figure 9.14 shows that Baby Superstore's stock was entrenched in a steady downtrend in spring 1996. They were scheduled to announce earnings the week of May 15. When that day came and went without an announcement, it set the stage for shorting the stock. The June 35 puts were trading for $2 1/4 at the time. More than a week passed before the company finally released their numbers, and they were as horrible as you'd expect. The stock collapsed on May 28, sending the puts above $10 intraday.

ANALYZE THE INDUSTRY BEFORE YOU BUY THE STOCK

Before you buy a stock, first examine its industry index to determine if the sector is in an up trend. You will increase your winning percentage because being in the right sector is just as (if not more) important than picking the right stock. Here's a simple technique you can use to quickly determine whether a sector is in a bullish mode and a stock purchase is advisable:

1. Calculate a 50-day moving average of the industry index.

2. Buy the stock only when the sector index closes above its 50-day moving average.

FIGURE 9.15

Analyze the Industry Before You Buy the Stock:
Intel (INTC) and the Semiconductor Index (SOX), Daily

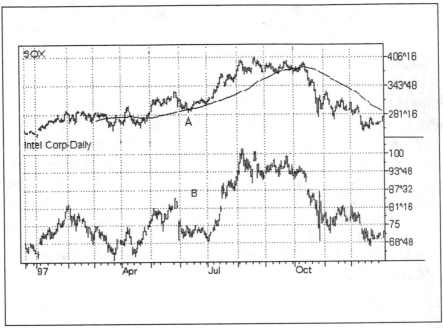

Source: Omega Research, Inc.

Figure 9.15 gives an example using Intel Corp., a leading
computer chip manufacturer, and the Semiconductor Index
(SOX), the index for that industry. The SOX index is gaining momentum at point A. At point B, Intel is just starting
to gain momentum. You would buy just in time for the up-
ward move in the stock. By doing this, you ensure you are
buying into an industry that is gaining momentum, rather
than focusing on what could turn out to be an aberration in
one stock.

CONCLUSION

Again, the emphasis on risk control and commonsense market behavior in these strategies is obvious. For the most part, once a trade is triggered, these strategies risk no more than the range of the current bar or the previous day's bar (which can be reduced in higher volatility situations when this risk may be too large). Trades are based on concrete market events: the natural pullback hot IPO stocks often experience soon after going public, the powerful moves that can result when a market doesn't react as expected to a news event. Acting quickly on specific price patterns and defining your risk immediately on each trade keeps the probabilities on your side and increases your trading profitability.

CHAPTER 10

What Top Traders Know

If you've done any reading on trading or the markets, you've undoubtedly come across dozens of "rules to live by"—pearls of wisdom intended to set your feet on the path to successful trading. Some of these rules (cut your losses short, let your profits run, for example) are undoubtedly sound advice, even if most beginners have to learn the truth of the matter the hard way. Other commonly accepted trading truths, however, are more suspect, and many actually fly in the face of smart trading.

Great traders learn their lessons in the arena that counts—the markets. They know that what feels comfortable—what feels "right"—is sometimes the wrong thing to do. What seems perfectly logical on paper can be actually illogical when you try to use it in real trading.

The strategies the TRADEHARD.COM cofounders have shared with you in the previous section are the products of real trading experience. What follows in this chapter are broader trading principles, observations, and rules that create the larger context for those strategies—realizations about market behavior these traders used as the basis for their approach.

MOMENTUM MONEY FRONT-RUNS THE MARKET

In the mid-1960s a Harvard Ph.D. candidate (who would become a well-known money manager) argued in his thesis that "momentum stocks" lead the market. This thesis has proved to be quite accurate over time.

The TRADEHARD.COM Momentum Index (TMI) is a proprietary indicator (recalculated every two or three days) that measures the performance of momentum stocks and helps exploit their leading characteristics. Especially important are those times when the Dow rises but the TMI drops. This tells us the market leaders did not participate in the rally—a tip-off that the overall market may drop over the next few days. The opposite reaction is implied when the Dow drops and the TMI rises; in these situations the "smart money" is buying, which will likely push the broader market higher over the next day or so.

Another way to measure momentum stock action is to put stocks with Relative Strength (RS) rankings of 98 and 99 in Investors Business Daily in a basket. (This information is also available on TRADEHARD.COM; the TMI uses a proprietary

FIGURE 10.1

Momentum Money Front-Runs the Market:
TMI and S&P 500, Daily

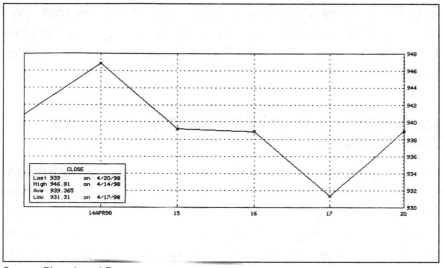

Source: Bloomberg LP.

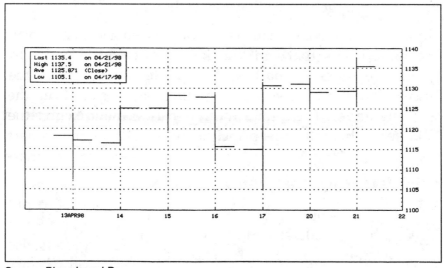

Source: Bloomberg LP.

mathematical formula to filter this list further). No matter how you calculate your index, update it frequently so it truly reflects recent market conditions. This will assure you of being able to measure the short-term health of the market. Figure 10.1 compares the TMI to the S&P 500 futures. Notice the up-and-down moves in the TMI precede similar moves in the S&P 500.

WINNING TRADES SHOULD STAY WINNERS

One of the major differences between traders who make a consistent living and everyone else is that they rarely allow profits to turn into losses. They do this by moving their stops to breakeven as soon as their trades generate a small profit. This, at worst, allows them to "scratch" their trades; it also keeps them in the market and allows them to participate in any large moves that may follow.

Good money management is simply common sense: Avoid the huge losers that can knock you out of the game for good; keep losses small, and don't let profits turn into losses. By definition, you'll be getting the most out of your winning trades. The 2-for-1 money management example in Chapter 9 illustrates this principle very well.

DOUBLING UP IS A LOSER'S GAME

Doubling up is buying 500 shares of a stock at 36 when you already bought 500 shares at 40, with the goal of lowering your break-even point to 38. This strategy has killed more traders than any other.

FIGURE 10.2

The Dangers of Doubling Up: Iomega (IOM), Weekly

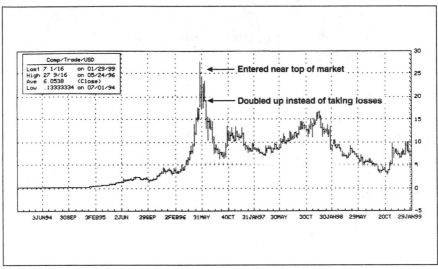

Source: Bloomberg LP.

Figure 10.2 tells the whole story. In early 1996, Iomega was the darling of many momentum traders and self-proclaimed Internet investment gurus. We know a trader who was unlucky enough—we're being kind—to have listened to these gurus and bought Iomega at 26 right before it peaked a little over 27 in the spring of 1996. Unfortunately, instead of taking his losses when the stock fell to 24, then 22, then 20, he doubled his position at 19 with the hope of breaking even on a rebound to 22 1/2. Unfortunately, as the chart shows, there was no bottom in site and this trader lost a big chunk of his net worth. A rule to live by: When a stock, futures contract, or option moves against you, *do not double up*. Take your losses and get out!

USE TRAILING STOPS TO LOCK IN PROFITS

Trailing stops are stop-loss orders that progress along with your position, moving higher when you are long, and moving lower when you are short. They are an effective and simple way to lock in profits. For example, assume you buy a stock at 34 and place your initial protective stop at 33. If the stock rises to 34 3/4, move your stop up to 34, guaranteeing at worst a scratch trade (less slippage and commis-

FIGURE 10.3

Trailing Stops: Yahoo (YHOO), Daily

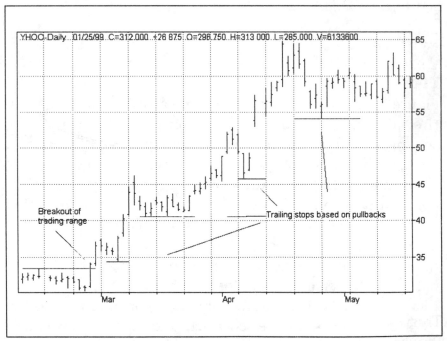

Source: Omega Research, Inc.

sions). When the stock rises to 35 1/2, raise your stop up to 34 1/2 or 34 3/4, and so on. You are essentially letting your profits run while assuring yourself of a winning trade.

The most credible piece of evidence supporting this strategy is that it is used by successful floor traders—it is the main reason why the best of them achieve such spectacular returns.

Figure 10.3 shows how a trailing stop might be applied in a rally. After an initial stop is placed to limit risk on the trade, you could use a trailing stop placed at the bottom of pullbacks (shown by the short horizontal lines). As the up trend progresses, you could use increasingly tighter stops tied to even smaller or shorter-term pullbacks.

YOU MUST MINIMIZE YOUR TRADING COSTS

Adhering to this principle will increase your returns by potentially thousands of dollars every year. The bottom line: You cannot trade successfully paying retail brokerage commissions. These inflated rates will eat into your potential profits almost as quickly as a string of bad trades. For example, if you trade once per day and pay $50 per trade rather than the $15 or less per-trade rate available through any number of online discount brokers, you will have $8,750 less in your trading account by the end of the year—a 17.5% loss on a $50,000 account!

This principle may seem like common sense, but tens of thousands of traders still pay higher retail commissions.

Find a good online discount firm—don't sacrifice your profits to make some broker rich.

IT'S NOT THE NUMBER OF WINNING TRADES, IT'S THE SIZE OF THE WINNERS THAT COUNTS

The general public believes successful traders make money every day—that 9 out of every 10 of their trades are winners. Nothing could be further from the truth. The reality is that in any given month most successful traders take small losses or gains on the majority of their trades, while their real money comes from a few trades that turn out to be big winners. By essentially "scratching" most of their trades they protect their capital, making it possible to wait patiently for the small handful of positions that turn into large gains.

Your trading results will skyrocket when you learn how to "scratch" trades and deal patiently with churning to participate in the moves that will bring you solid returns.

KEEP AN EYE ON LEVERAGE

While leverage can be one of the most useful tools at the disposal of the futures trader, it's important to understand it fully and keep it in perspective. Once you decide on a trading system or approach, you must consider how many contracts or shares to trade per signal, and the maximum number to hold at any point in time. After conducting historical tests, consider the following:

Maximum drawdown. This is the largest peak-to-valley equity decline in dollar terms. Many beginning traders use this figure to calculate the number of contracts to trade—that is, they capitalize their accounts equal to the maximum drawdown, thinking that is all the capital they will need to trade. Unfortunately, historical drawdown figures are usually exceeded in real trading because the longer a system is exposed to the markets, the more negative market events it will encounter. A more realistic estimate is to double the maximum drawdown generated in historical testing and base the number of contracts you trade on this figure.

Absolute Leverage. This figure is a simple, but statistically robust, calculation that is surprisingly absent from most historical testing software. Absolute leverage is calculated by dividing the total dollar value of all the contracts you hold by your current account equity. As a rule of thumb, you should be very cautious about exceeding a five-to-one absolute leverage ratio. Drawdowns in these situations usually become very large and most traders cannot survive them.

DIVERSIFICATION MEANS MORE THAN JUST MULTIPLE MARKETS

While many traders think diversification essentially means trading a handful of "unrelated" stocks or futures contracts, it takes a little more to truly reduce risk in your portfolio. Because even supposedly unrelated markets will be highly correlated during extreme periods (consider the plunges many commodities took the day of the 1987 stock market crash), it helps to trade different kinds of systems or different versions of the same system to spread your risk.

An example would be for long-term trend-following traders to add shorter-term countertrend or swing systems to their repertoire and also use multiple versions of their standard trend system—vary the number of days, or use altered confirmation rules that change the sensitivity of the system. Because the drawdowns of these different approaches are much less likely to occur at the same time, your equity curve will be smoother. Lower risk trading means lower capital requirements, so the percentage return should be increased. Manuel Ochoa illustrated the benefits of this technique in his chapter on system design and testing.

These system and time frame diversification techniques also enable traders active in only a handful of markets to reduce their risk.

THE #1 BEST ADVICE WE CAN GIVE YOU—WHEN YOU'RE WRONG, GET THE HELL OUT!

Don't fight the market! It sounds simple, but one of the hardest things for traders to do is to stop trying to impose their wills on the market. Virtually every successful trader ever interviewed has said that learning how to take losses (and keep them small) was one of the most important accomplishments in his career. Professional trading is about being realistic, and as we have noted, the reality of trading is that you have to sit through several small losing trades for every one of the big winners that will ultimately pay the bills.

Just think about the trade examples from the strategies section: Jeff Cooper never risks more than one point on a trade; Kevin Haggerty never risks more than 3/8 of a point intraday. The reality is, when they put on a trade, they feel it should immediately move in their favor. *If it doesn't, they get out.*

The desire to hold on to losing trades (in the hope they will become winners) is a characteristic of novice traders, and more often than not, it's not just about the pain of losing money, it's about the pain of admitting you're wrong. Too many would-be traders go into the markets to prove how smart they are—how well they can "call" the market.

But trading is not about proving how smart you are, it's about making money. In fact, the desire to prove how smart you are can keep you from entering profitable trades or keep you stuck in losing ones because doing otherwise would conflict with your market bias. If your analysis has convinced you the market is due for a bull move, for example, you may overlook a change in the character of the market and avoid taking an obvious sell signal.

Don't try to forecast markets, try to understand them. Then, develop a trading plan that reflects this understanding and reacts to price action—as it develops— accordingly. Do what the market is telling you to do. (Any trading system worth its salt should do this for you automatically.) Professional traders do not stay "married" to market opinions or trades out of pride. You shouldn't, either. Keep your ego out of it

One very tangible rule in this area: *Never* move a stop farther away from the market after you've placed it. If you're going to move a stop, move it closer to your position (see the discussion on trailing stops earlier in the chapter).

CONCLUSION

Part of developing or using good trading strategies and being a profitable trader is having an understanding of how markets really work. While many of the principles described in this chapter may seem obvious or simple, they are the kinds of things that distinguish professionals who make their livings in the markets from everyone else. The trick is to make such knowledge part of your trading approach, not just something you read about in a book.

CHAPTER 11

Reaching the Trading Pinnacle

Popular perceptions notwithstanding, great traders aren't born, they're made—through experience. The realism and discipline that come from experience allows top traders to prosper over the long haul and avoid the land mines that blow away so many unwary market soldiers. The question is, what are the most important lessons top traders have learned from their campaigns?

It's often amazing how many great traders—despite their diverse approaches—seem to have taken such similar lessons out of their trading experiences. Although there are any number of techniques you can use to profit in the markets—short-term, long-term, methods specifically for stocks, futures, or options—there are a handful of fundamental principles that seem to unite all *successful* market players.

First, they accept how markets really work. They know markets are driven by tangible, understandable factors like human emotion (greed and fear), the interaction between different institutional players, and overall economic climate—not mysterious, mystical forces.

Second, they develop strategies that allow them to exploit these kinds of market characteristics. When you know what drives markets, you learn how they tend to react to certain events—the release of big news items, a pullback after a hot IPO, a pause in a trend, an initial breakout of a new high or low—and how to identify the patterns that give you an edge in the market.

Third, they trade both sides of the market. Exclusively trading the long side of the market, especially in stocks, is an amateur's approach. Professionals realize they need strategies to buy or sell, depending on the circumstances, or strategies (like some of the techniques in the options chapter) that work no matter which direction the market is going.

Finally, and most importantly, they use tight risk control and money management that keeps losing trades small and makes the most out of winners. Every successful trader stresses the importance of money management over specific trade triggers. They never risk too much on one trade, and they never let a small loss turn into a big one. Using tight stops to limit initial risk and following up with trailing stops that lock in profits are typical money management approaches for professional traders.

Not surprisingly, these are precisely the ideas and techniques that appear in chapter after chapter of this book.

These principles are not about "holy grail" trading systems or million-dollar overnight windfalls. They are what real traders have learned about making real money in the markets. Consider Kevin Haggerty's strategies for exploiting the interaction of institutions and specialists in the stock market, and his use of half-point or smaller stops for his intraday trades; or Jeff Cooper's techniques that key off large bids in thin markets or pullbacks of hot IPOs; or any of the other techniques that isolate specific aspects of market behavior (volatility explosions, the herd mentality, etc.) and capitalize on them with quick-acting, low-risk patterns. Mark Boucher's chapter on risk control, which singles out money management as the most important element of successful trading, simply reflects the approach of all the traders and all the strategies throughout the book.

Successful trading is never effortless or without risk; it's hard work. But it doesn't have to be complicated. Sound market logic, practical trading ideas, no-nonsense risk control: These are the keys to successful trading and the lessons of *The TRADEHARD.COM Guide to Conquering the Trading Markets.*

The New Trading Technology and the TRADEHARD.COM Web site

All facets of the trading industry have become increasingly digital over the past decade, and the trend shows no sign of slowing. Electronic exchanges and broker networks have steadily encroached on the turf of the traditional open outcry exchanges. More price data and analysis services offer their products directly over the Internet, and online brokerages that allow customers to enter trades directly on the Internet are flourishing. We'll take a look at what these developments mean for you as a trader and how to best stay on top of the continually evolving market environment.

ELECTRONIC EXCHANGES

The traditional trading floor of crowded, noisy trading pits, flashing quote boards, and flying pieces of paper is being challenged by computer exchanges and electronic networks. These "virtual exchanges" threaten to supersede floor brokers and traders as the most efficient and cost-effective method of matching buyers and sellers. While a complete conversion of the industry may still be many years off (the traditional exchanges still have a great deal of political and financial clout), electronic exchanges have moved beyond their maverick roots and established themselves as financial powers and prototypes for the trading industry's future.

Most stock traders have probably been part of an electronic "exchange" without ever having thought much about it. The NASDAQ (National Association of Securities Dealers Automated Quotations), while not a true exchange, is the largest stock market in the country, outpacing the volume on the NYSE by many millions of shares on an average day. The Nasdaq is home to many of the leading technology and Internet stocks, including companies like Microsoft, Intel, Apple, Amazon.com, and Yahoo. While it used to be called the OTC ("over-the-counter") market, the Nasdaq is now a market with listing standards, trading surveillance, real-time price reporting, etc. It uses an electronic screen-based network to disseminate bid, ask, and last sale information to dealers. There's no trading floor, and no one ever meets face to face to make a trade.

The Nasdaq uses a multiple market maker system, whereby securities dealers compete with each other for investor orders. The best bids and offers are displayed on the network, and dealers around the world can buy and sell accordingly. A true computerized exchange goes a step further. A central computer system automatically matches all customer bids and offers, which can be placed through licensed trade entry terminals. One of the most formidable of these new exchanges is the Eurex (formerly the Deutsche Terminborse), Germany's computerized exchange for stock index, interest rate, and currency futures. It has superseded the London International Financial Futures and Options Exchange (LIFFE, the dominant European financial futures exchange) as the primary market for the important German Bund (long-term government bond) only a few years after it began trading the contract.

Computerized exchanges promise the ability to remove human error from the trade-matching process and offer a less-expensive trading alternative by reducing the need for middle-men brokers and the high overhead associated with traditional trading floors. Recently, some brokerages, sensing the potential of electronic trading networks and exchanges, have successfully launched virtual exchanges of their own—institutions that are directly challenging the hegemony of today's major exchanges (who, not surprisingly, tried to use their influence to prevent such exchanges from seeing the light of day).

But even established open outcry exchanges themselves have begun to offer electronic alternatives to their trading pits in the hopes of increasing volume in illiquid instruments or capitalizing on customers interested in trading during off-hours. In the not-too-distant future, trading may truly be available around the clock, as traders and investors are routinely able to perform their analysis, enter trades, and receive confirmations directly from their computers.

What does this mean to you? Actually, not much in terms of analysis and developing your own trading approach (other than changes a true 24-hour trading day may necessitate). Licensed brokers are still the only people who can execute trades; the only difference on your end is how you communicate with your broker—online versus over the phone, for example. The advent of the Internet and online technical analysis and trade entry is the final piece of the puzzle

THE ROLE OF THE INTERNET

The Internet's natural ability to provide inexpensive access to multiple types of information is perfectly suited to trading. While many other industries are still trying to figure out what the Internet is all about and how it can help them, the financial industry is already offering a cutting-edge menu of valuable information and services to its consumers.

The combination of stand-alone technical analysis software and price data purchased from a vendor has been the most common arrangement for individual technical traders in recent years. The Internet, however, promises to replace the traditional setup because it can provide online analysis tools, real-time and historical data, news and other financial information, online trade entry, portfolio monitoring, and other trading resources in a single package.

Online brokerages that let you enter orders over the Internet (usually at a deep discount to traditional brokerage) are proliferating. There also are sites dedicated to technical analysis and trading strategies, financial information on companies, market news and commentary—even trading system testing. Virtually every exchange in the world has its own Web site, offering valuable information about the instruments they trade as well as quotes and price histories. What all these varied enterprises take advantage of is the opportunity to provide instant access to information and services in a wide variety of formats—real-time price data, historical price data, technical analysis and system testing tools, trade transmission, interactive discussion, online articles, interviews and instructional "texts," live or delayed audio and video, and product purchases.

What has been missing, however, is a site that integrates all the features and all the possibilities outlined above.

THE TRADEHARD.COM WEB SITE

The purpose of the TRADEHARD.COM Web site is to take advantage of the possibilities of the Internet by offering constantly updated professional trading indicators, market commentary, prices quotes and portfolio tracking, live interactive seminars with top traders, educational materials, message boards, and a host of other analysis resources and trading support. We support this comprehensive online trading community and resource center with informative books that help you maximize its potential.

Instead of selecting a piece of analysis software from one company, finding price data from another, and sifting through dozens of books for fragments of useful trading information, we offer "one-stop-shopping" for traders interested in market insights and techniques from professional traders rather than armchair analysts or self-proclaimed market gurus. We specialize in detailed, proprietary content designed to help you buck the trading herd—not get stampeded along with it.

Proprietary Market Indicators

Our Web site provides numerous original technical indicators, updated daily or weekly, for stock, futures, and option traders, designed by traders to give you practical, powerful tools to use in the markets—not the standard laundry list of indicators found on every other site and software program. Among the bases we cover: proprietary relative strength rankings and lists of the strongest and weakest stocks, stock sectors, and futures; customized relative strength scans; cup-and-handle patterns and pullbacks; key volatility measurements to identify potential markets explosions; market bias indicators; breakout candidates, and lists of the most over- and under-priced stock and futures options. These are only some of the indicator resources you can tap into on a daily basis.

Market Commentary and Updates

In addition to the stable of proprietary indicators, we also provide timely commentary on the stock and futures markets throughout the day from professional traders who tell you where the trading action is and what the best trading opportunities are. We provide a pre-opening market report, an intraday report, and a wrap-up after the close every day.

In addition to the intraday commentary and analysis, we also offer a rotating schedule of weekly updates and commentaries from the TRADEHARD.COM cofounders focusing on different aspects of the stock, futures, and option markets. Also, our Technology Insight and Medical Technology Insight sections offer insider perspectives from high-tech and medical professionals who have their fingers on the pulses of these industries. You'll find out which companies in these hot stock sectors will be the tomorrow's giants and which will be also-rans.

Trader Forums and Message Boards

Trading can often be a lonely business—just you and your computer screen. It always helps to be able to bounce ideas off other traders. You'll get the opportunity to go one-on-one with professional traders through our live Trader Forums. You'll have direct access to great trading minds and the opportunity to ask the kinds of questions you've always wanted answers to but rarely come across in print interviews.

Along with the Trader Forums, our message boards provide the perfect forum for exchanging trading ideas, tips, and questions with other traders—24 hours a day.

Educational Resources: Articles and Interviews

TRADEHARD.COM also offers an always-expanding menu of educational articles for beginning traders, strategy articles for advanced traders and hedge fund managers, and in-depth interviews with top traders—more concrete trading information than you'll find in any number of so-called trader magazines.

Quotes, Charts, and News

In addition to our first-rate proprietary content, TRADEHARD.COM offers a full array of quotes, charts, news, economic data, and portfolio tracking. You'll be able to stay on top of every tick of the markets throughout the day.

CONCLUSION

Global markets and instantaneous digital communications make staying on top of the latest technological developments critical for competitive trading. Knowing how to use the latest Internet technologies and online resources—how you can get more information, get it quicker, and save money—gives you a definite edge in the markets.

Other Books from
M. GORDON
PUBLISHING GROUP
www.mgordonpub.com

STREET SMARTS
High Probability Short-Term Trading Strategies

LAURENCE A. CONNORS AND LINDA BRADFORD RASCHKE

Published in 1996 and written by Larry Connors and *New Market Wizard* Linda Raschke, this 245-page manual is considered by many to be one of the best books written on trading futures. Twenty-five years of combined trading experience is divulged as you will learn 20 of their best strategies. Among the methods you will be taught are:

- **Swing Trading** The backbone of Linda's success. Not only will you learn exactly how to swing trade, you will also learn specific advanced techniques never before made public.

- **News**—Among the strategies revealed is an intraday news strategy they use to exploit the herd when the 8:30 A.M. economic reports are released. This strategy will be especially appreciated by bond traders and currency traders.

- **Pattern Recognition**—You will learn some of the best short-term setup patterns available. Larry and Linda will also teach you how they combine these patterns with other strategies to identify explosive moves.

- **ADX**—In our opinion, ADX is one of the most powerful and misunderstood indicators available to traders. Now, for the first time, they reveal a handful of short-term trading strategies they use in conjunction with this terrific indicator.

- **Volatility**—You will learn how to identify markets that are about to explode and how to trade these exciting situations.

- Also, included are chapters on trading the smart money index, trading Crabel, trading gap reversals, a special chapter on professional money management, and many other trading strategies!

245 PAGES HARD COVER $175.00

HIT AND RUN TRADING
The Short-Term Stock Traders' Bible

JEFF COOPER

Written by professional equities trader, Jeff Cooper, this best-selling manual teaches traders how to day-trade and short-term trade stocks. Jeff's strategies identify daily the ideal stocks to trade and point out the exact entry and protective exit point. Most trades risk 1 point or less and last from a few hours to a few days.

Among the strategies taught are:

- Stepping In Front Of Size—You will be taught how to identify when a large institution is desperately attempting to buy or sell a large block of stock. You will then be taught how to step in front of this institution before the stock explodes or implodes. This strategy many times leads to gains from 1/4 point to 4 points within minutes.

- 1-2-3-4s—Rapidly moving stocks tend to pause for a few days before they explode again. You will be taught the three-day setup that consistently triggers solid gains within days.

- Expansion Breakouts—Most breakouts are false! You will learn the one breakout pattern that consistently leads to further gains. This pattern alone is worth the price of the manual.

- Also, you will learn how to trade market explosions (Boomers), how to trade secondary offerings, how to trade Slingshots, and you will learn a number of other profitable strategies that will make you a stronger trader.

160 PAGES HARD COVER $100.00

HIT AND RUN TRADING II
CAPTURING EXPLOSIVE SHORT-TERM MOVES IN STOCKS

JEFF COOPER

212 fact-filled pages of new trading strategies from Jeff Cooper. You will learn the best momentum continuation and reversal strategies to trade. You will also be taught the best day-trading strategies that have allowed Jeff to make his living trading for the past decade. Also included is a special five-chapter bonus section entitled, "Techniques of a Professional Trader" where Jeff teaches you the most important aspects of trading, including money management, stop placement, daily preparation, and profit-taking strategies.

If you aspire to become a full-time professional trader, this is the book for you.

212 PAGES HARD COVER $100.00

THE 5-DAY MOMENTUM METHOD

JEFF COOPER

Strongly trending stocks always pause before they resume their move. *The 5-Day Momentum Method* identifies three- to seven-day explosive moves on strongly trending momentum stocks. Highly recommended for traders who are looking for larger than normal short-term gains and who do not want to sit in front of the screen during the day. *The 5-Day Momentum Method* works as well shorting declining stocks as it does buying rising stocks. Also, there is a special section written for option traders.

SPIRAL BOUND $50.00

INVESTMENT SECRETS OF A HEDGE FUND MANAGER
Exploiting the Herd Mentality of the Financial Markets

LAURENCE A. CONNORS AND BLAKE E. HAYWARD

Released in 1995, this top-selling trading book reveals strategies that give you the tools to stand apart from the crowd.

Among the strategies you will learn from this book are:

- **Connors-Hayward Historical Volatility System**—The most powerful chapter in the book, this revolutionary method utilizes historical volatility to pinpoint markets that are ready to explode.

- **News Reversals**—A rule-based strategy to exploit the irrational crowd psychology caused by news events.

- **NDX-SPX**—An early-warning signal that uses the NASDAQ 100 Index to anticipate moves in the S&P 500.

- **Globex**—Cutting edge techniques that identify mispricings that regularly occur on the Globex markets.

225 PAGES CLOTH COVER $49.95

CONNORS ON ADVANCED TRADING STRATEGIES
31 Chapters on Beating the Markets

LAURENCE A. CONNORS

Written by Larry Connors, this new book is broken into seven sections; S&P and stock market timing, volatility, new patterns, equities, day-trading, options, and more advanced trading strategies and concepts. Thirty-one chapters of in-depth knowledge to bring you up to the same level of trading as the professionals.

Among the strategies you will learn are:

- **Connors VIX Reversals I, II and III (Chapter 2)**—Three of the most powerful strategies ever revealed. You will learn how the CBOE OEX Volatility Index (VIX) pinpoints short-term highs and lows in the S&Ps and the stock market. The average profit/trade for this method is among the highest Larry has ever released.

- **The 15 Minute ADX Breakout Method (Chapter 20)**— Especially for day-traders! This dynamic method teaches you how to specifically trade the most explosive futures and stocks everyday! This strategy alone is worth the price of the book.

- **Options (Section 5)**—Four chapters and numerous in-depth strategies for trading options. You will learn the strategies used by the best Market Makers and a small handful of professionals to consistently capture options gains!

- **Crash, Burn, and Profit (Chapter 11)**—Huge profits occur when stocks implode. During a recent 12-month period, the Crash, Burn and Profit strategy shorted Centennial Technologies at 49 1/8; six weeks later it was at 2 1/2! It shorted Diana Corp. at 67 3/8; a few months later it collapsed to 4 3/8! It recently shorted Fine Host at 35; eight weeks later the stock was halted from trading at 10! This strategy will be an even bigger bonanza for you in a bear market.

- **Advanced Volatility Strategies (Section 2)**—Numerous, never-before revealed strategies and concepts using volatility to identify markets immediately before they explode.

- and much, much more!

259 PAGES HARD COVER $150.00

METHOD IN DEALING IN STOCKS
Reading the Mind of the Market on a Daily Basis

JOSEPH H. KERR, JR.

This gem was originally published in 1931 by Joseph Kerr has been expanded and updated to reflect today's markets. This book is considered to be the bible of interpreting both daily market action and daily news events.

150 PAGES PAPERBACK $35.00

THE BEST OF THE PROFESSIONAL TRADERS JOURNAL SERIES

Best Trading Patterns: Volume I

Best Trading Patterns: Volume II

Market Timing

Options Trading and Volatility Trading

Day Trading

EACH VOLUME $39.95

used by the best Market Makers and a small handful of professionals to consistently capture options gains!

- **Crash, Burn, and Profit (Chapter 11)**—Huge profits occur when stocks implode. During a recent 12-month period, the Crash, Burn and Profit strategy shorted Centennial Technologies at 49 1/8; six weeks later it was at 2 1/2! It shorted Diana Corp. at 67 3/8; a few months later it collapsed to 4 3/8! It recently shorted Fine Host at 35; eight weeks later the stock was halted from trading at 10! This strategy will be an even bigger bonanza for you in a bear market.

- **Advanced Volatility Strategies (Section 2)**—Numerous, never-before revealed strategies and concepts using volatility to identify markets immediately before they explode.

- and much, much more!

259 PAGES HARD COVER $150.00

METHOD IN DEALING IN STOCKS
Reading the Mind of the Market on a Daily Basis

JOSEPH H. KERR, JR.

This gem was originally published in 1931 by Joseph Kerr has been expanded and updated to reflect today's markets. This book is considered to be the bible of interpreting both daily market action and daily news events.

150 PAGES PAPERBACK $35.00

THE BEST OF THE PROFESSIONAL TRADERS JOURNAL SERIES

Best Trading Patterns: Volume I

Best Trading Patterns: Volume II

Market Timing

Options Trading and Volatility Trading

Day Trading

EACH VOLUME $39.95